The FLAMES ™

Celebrating Calgary's Dream Season, 2003-04

THE FLAMES ®
Celebrating Calgary's Dream Season, 2003-04

A Fenn Publishing Book / First Published in 2004

Fenn Publishing Company Ltd.
Bolton, Ontario, Canada

Library and Archives Canada Cataloguing in Publication
Podnieks, Andrew
The Flames : celebrating Calgary's dream season / Andrew Podnieks.
ISBN 1-55168-269-9

1. Calgary Flames (Hockey team) 2. Stanley Cup (Hockey) I. Title.

GV848.C28P62 2004   796.962'64'09712338   C2004-903492-8

Acknowledgements
The author would like to thank the few but important people who helped put this book together both quickly and
carefully. First, to publisher Jordan Fenn for his confidence in the project and the resulting enthusiasm he brought
to its completion. Next, to Jefferson Davis and Angus Gillespie for helping to write some of the game stories for
the regular season (Jeff) and playoffs (Angus). To the design team at First Image (www.fiwired.com), Michael
Gray and Rob Scanlan, for bringing their many years of imagination and experience to bear on a book that took
scarcely two weeks to produce. Also, to George Puro of the NHL for providing league endorsement of the project.
Lastly, to Nancy Glowinski at Reuters and Glenn Levy at BBS for their quick and kind help with all the photos.
To all, a great thanks for a job well done.

Photo Credits
All photos—front and back cover and interior—courtesy of REUTERS, with the following exceptions
from Bruce Bennett Studios (BBS): pages 9, 15, 19, 26, 30, 31, 32, 37, 42 (both), 43.

Designed by First Image

Distributed in Canada by H. B. Fenn and Company Ltd.
Bolton, Ontario, Canada, L7E 1W2
www.hbfenn.com

Printed in Canada

AN OFFICIAL STANLEY CUP® PUBLICATION

The FLAMES™

Celebrating Calgary's Dream Season, 2003-04

Andrew Podnieks

FENN

Fenn Publishing Company Ltd.

Contents

Introduction vi

The Organization 8

Birth of the Calgary Flames 9

Training Camp Roster and Player Movement . 10

All Regular Season Games, 2003-04 12-53

October 9, 2003	Calgary 1 at Vancouver 4	12
October 11, 2003	San Jose 2 at Calgary 3	12
October 14, 2003	Edmonton 0 at Calgary 1	12
October 18, 2003	Buffalo 2 at Calgary 0	13
October 21, 2003	Calgary 3 at Minnesota 2	14
October 24, 2003	St. Louis 2 at Calgary 1	14
October 25, 2003	Calgary 4 at Edmonton 2	14
October 28, 2003	Calgary 2 at Colorado 4	15
October 29, 2003	Calgary 3 at Dallas 4	16
November 1, 2003	Columbus 0 at Calgary 3	16
November 4, 2003	Detroit 3 at Calgary 0	17
November 7, 2003	Minnesota 3 at Calgary 0	17
November 9, 2003	Calgary 3 at Columbus 4	18
November 12, 2003	Calgary 6 at Chicago 2	18
November 13, 2003	Calgary 1 at Nashville 4	19
November 15, 2003	Calgary 1 at Edmonton 2	19
November 18, 2003	Toronto 2 at Calgary 3	20
November 20, 2003	Montreal 1 at Calgary 2	20
November 22, 2003	Chicago 1 at Calgary 2	21
November 27, 2003	Colorado 6 at Calgary 5	21
November 29, 2003	Vancouver 4 at Calgary 4	22
December 2, 2003	San Jose 1 at Calgary 3	22
December 4, 2003	Calgary 4 at Vancouver 1	22
December 5, 2003	Minnesota 1 at Calgary 2	23
December 7, 2003	Pittsburgh 1 at Calgary 6	24
December 9, 2003	Calgary 1 at Minnesota 2	24
December 11, 2003	Carolina 0 at Calgary 1	24
December 13, 2003	Colorado 1 at Calgary 1	25
December 16, 2003	Calgary 3 at Philadelphia 2	26
December 18, 2003	Calgary 5 at Boston 0	26
December 19, 2003	Calgary 2 at Columbus 1	27
December 23, 2003	Edmonton 1 at Calgary 2	27
December 26, 2003	Vancouver 2 at Calgary 0	28
December 28, 2003	Calgary 2 at Edmonton 1	28
December 29, 2003	Minnesota 2 at Calgary 2	28
December 31, 2003	Colorado 2 at Calgary 1	29
January 3, 2004	Vancouver 3 at Calgary 1	30
January 5, 2004	Calgary 5 at Rangers 0	30
January 6, 2004	Calgary 3 at Islanders 2	31
January 8, 2004	Calgary 1 at Chicago 3	31
January 10, 2004	Florida 2 at Calgary 4	32
January 13, 2004	Calgary 1 at Toronto 4	32
January 14, 2004	Calgary 3 at Washington 3	32
January 17, 2004	Dallas 3 at Calgary 2	33
January 19, 2004	Calgary 5 at Anaheim 1	34
January 20, 2004	Calgary 1 at Los Angeles 4	34
January 22, 2004	Nashville 0 at Calgary 4	34
January 24, 2004	Tampa Bay 6 at Calgary 2	35
January 27, 2004	Calgary 2 at Phoenix 1	36
January 28, 2004	Calgary 1 at San Jose 4	36
January 30, 2004	Chicago 5 at Calgary 3	37
February 1, 2004	Anaheim 4 at Calgary 6	37
February 3, 2004	Los Angeles 4 at Calgary 4	38
February 5, 2004	St. Louis 2 at Calgary 1	38
	54th NHL All-Star Game	39
February 10, 2004	Atlanta 2 at Calgary 5	40
February 11, 2004	Calgary 3 at Vancouver 2	40
February 13, 2004	Anaheim 1 at Calgary 2	40
February 15, 2004	Calgary 2 at Minnesota 1	41
February 19, 2004	Calgary 1 at Montreal 4	42
February 21, 2004	Calgary 1 at Ottawa 2	42
February 22, 2004	Calgary 1 at New Jersey 3	42
February 24, 2004	Calgary 2 at Colorado 0	43
February 26, 2004	Detroit 2 at Calgary 1	44
February 29, 2004	Phoenix 2 at Calgary 4	44
March 2, 2004	Calgary 4 at St. Louis 2	44
March 3, 2004	Calgary 1 at Detroit 2	45
March 5, 2004	Calgary 1 at Dallas 5	46
March 7, 2004	Calgary 7 at Colorado 1	46
March 9, 2004	Edmonton 1 at Calgary 1	47
March 11, 2004	Ottawa 2 at Calgary 4	47
March 13, 2004	Calgary 4 at Nashville 4	48
March 14, 2004	Calgary 3 at St. Louis 0	48
March 16, 2004	Calgary 4 at Detroit 1	49
March 18, 2004	Columbus 0 at Calgary 2	49
March 20, 2004	Nashville 3 at Calgary 1	50
March 22, 2004	Dallas 4 at Calgary 0	50
March 24, 2004	Calgary 4 at Phoenix 0	51
March 25, 2004	Calgary 2 at San Jose 3	51
March 27, 2004	Los Angeles 2 at Calgary 3	52
March 31, 2004	Phoenix 0 at Calgary 1	52
April 2, 2004	Calgary 3 at Los Angeles 2	52
April 4, 2004	Calgary 1 at Anaheim 2	53

Final NHL Standings & Flames Statistics,
   Regular Season 55

All 2004 NHL Playoff Results 55

Final Flames Statistics 56

How the Team Was Built 57

Flames' Playoff Story, 2004 58-107

Conference Quarter-Finals:
Calgary Flames vs. Vancouver Canucks . 58-71

April 7, 2004	Calgary 3 at Vancouver 5	58
April 9, 2004	Calgary 2 at Vancouver 1	60
April 11, 2004	Vancouver 2 at Calgary 1	62
April 13, 2004	Vancouver 0 at Calgary 4	64
April 15, 2004	Calgary 2 at Vancouver 1	66
April 17, 2004	Vancouver 5 at Calgary 4	68
April 19, 2004	Calgary 3 at Vancouver 2	70

Conference Semi-Finals:
Calgary Flames vs. Detroit Red Wings . . 72-83

April 22, 2004	Calgary 2 at Detroit 1	72
April 24, 2004	Calgary 2 at Detroit 5	74
April 27, 2004	Detroit 2 at Calgary 3	76
April 29, 2004	Detroit 4 at Calgary 2	78
May 1, 2004	Calgary 1 at Detroit 0	80
May 3, 2004	Detroit 0 at Calgary 1	82

Conference Finals:
Calgary Flames vs. San Jose Sharks 84-95

May 9, 2004	Calgary 4 at San Jose 3	84
May 11, 2004	Calgary 4 at San Jose 1	86
May 13, 2004	San Jose 3 at Calgary 0	88
May 16, 2004	San Jose 4 at Calgary 2	90
May 17, 2004	Calgary 3 at San Jose 0	92
May 19, 2004	San Jose 1 at Calgary 3	94

STANLEY CUP FINALS:
Calgary Flames vs. Tampa Bay Lightning 96-109

May 25, 2004	Calgary 4 at Tampa Bay 1	96
May 27, 2004	Calgary 1 at Tampa Bay 4	98
May 29, 2004	Tampa Bay 0 at Calgary 3	100
May 31, 2004	Tampa Bay 1 at Calgary 0	102
June 3, 2004	Calgary 3 at Tampa Bay 2	104
June 5, 2004	Tampa Bay 3 at Calgary 2	106
June 7, 2004	Calgary 1 at Tampa Bay 2	108

Recalling the 1988-89 Calgary Flames 110

Trophy Winners/Retired Numbers/Captains/
Coaches/GM's/All-Star Team Selections . . 112

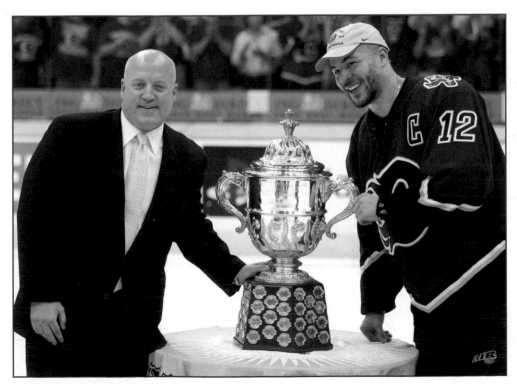

Bill Daly of the NHL presents captain Jarome Iginla with the Clarence S. Campbell Bowl after Calgary's six-game elimination of San Jose.

Vancouver's Artem Chubarov congratulates goalie Miikka Kiprusoff at the end of Game 7 of the Conference Quarter-Finals in Vancouver, won by the Flames, 3-2, in overtime.

Introduction

Who could believe now, in June 2004, that the Calgary Flames would have had the season they had! Who could have anticipated the team playing Game 7 of a the Stanley Cup Finals? Who could have predicted the Tampa Bay Lightning would be their opponent? It has, indeed, been a dream season for the Flames, one that started out in training camp like so many before, full of some promise and cautious optimism, concerns about finances, touting of young talent, and hopes to make the playoffs for the first time since 1996.

And then the start of the season merely confirmed all of the above. Goaltending was a concern. Could Roman Turek bounce back and have an excellent season? Well, he got hurt early, twice, and all of a sudden the number-one man was Jamie McLennan. He deserves honourable mention for his early contributions, for settling the team down, for giving the team quality, number-one-like goaltending until the arrival of Miikka Kiprusoff.

In the early going, the season went as expected. Through the first 16 games, the Flames were a weak 6-10-0 and everyone struggled with accepting another middling year with a finish out of the playoffs. But coach Darryl Sutter never panicked. He never went from game to game helter skelter. It was, after all, a long season.

If there was an early turning point, it would have to be a pair of home wins against Toronto, 3-2, and Montreal two nights later, 2-1. These were huge wins, impressive wins, wins that gave the team confidence and momentum. These were the first back-to-back wins since games two and three of the first week of the season. They were wins against teams that had as many of their own fans in Calgary as the hometown Flames, wins against Canada's two Original Six teams.

Over the course of the next 19 games, the Flames' record was 13-3-3. They established solid footing in the top eight of the Western Conference, playoff territory. In that stretch, they also beat Philadelphia, 3-2, and Vancouver, 4-1. They tied the Avalanche 1-1 and lost a thrilling second game to Colorado, 6-5. They were playing quality hockey.

The rest of the season was consistently above .500 for the Flames. In February, they had a modest four-game winning streak, but more impressive they never got on a losing streak of any length, either. They acquired Kiprusoff from San Jose, and when given the chance he proved himself not just a good goaltender but a great one, a Stanley Cup goalie. Perhaps the highlight of the season was a 7-1 win over Colorado in Denver. Perhaps it was the fact that the Flames registered eleven shutouts in 82 games, testament to their superb defensive play.

The team also played exciting hockey, open hockey that counted goals as important as defensive systems. Captain Jarome Iginla led the team. In the early going, when he was in a slump, so, too, was the team. As he got his rhythm, the team started to win, and by season's end he was a co-winner of the "Rocket" Richard Trophy with 41 goals, the second time he's led the league in goal scoring.

After Kiprusoff and Iginla, though, the entire team played well and each player made his contribution to the team's development and success. Martin Gelinas was the playoff hero, scoring three successive series-clinching goals. Craig Conroy scored timely goals and was a fiend at both ends of the ice. Shean Donovan and Stephane Yelle stepped up and new-comers made an impact. Rookie Matt Lombardi established himself as an NHLer and Robyn Regehr matured. The team's blueline suffered injuries, but the replacements came in and did an outstanding job, no more so than Mike Commodore, who played well inside his own blueline and made this group of players more like a "team" by stylizing his hair into an orange afro that was as photogenic as any great goal the team scored! And who will ever forget the playoff run of '04 that featured the Flames' popular beard-growing contest and nightly parades along the Red Mile after every game!

And so, this is a celebration of a great season made possible by a group of players that developed steadily into a great team. They played well, grew confident, and went on a wild ride in the playoffs that saw the Calgary Flames go to Game 7 of the Stanley Cup Finals. Amazing.

The Organization

OWNERS
Murray Edwards, Harley Hotchkiss, Alvin Libin, Allan Markin, Bud McCaig, Clayton Riddell, Byron Seaman, Daryl Seaman

EXECUTIVE
Ken King	President & CEO
Darryl Sutter	Head coach & GM
Michael Holditch	Vice President, Hockey Administration
Libby Raines	Vice President, Building Operations
Jim Bagshaw	Vice President, Advertising, Sponsorship, Marketing
Rollie Cyr	Vice President, Sales & Ticket Operations
Jim Peplinski	Vice President, Business Development

TEAM PERSONNEL
Darryl Sutter	Head coach & GM
Michael Holditch	Vice President, Hockey Administration
Mike Burke	Director, Hockey Administration
Al MacNeil	Special Assistant to GM
Jim Playfair	Assistant Coach
Rich Preston	Assistant Coach
Rob Cookson	Assistant Coach
Jamie Hislop	Development Coach
David Marcoux	Goaltending Coach
Brenda Koyich	Executive Assistant to GM & Hockey Operations
Kelly Chesla	Team Services Manager
Tod Button	Director of Scouting
Mike Sands	Director of Amateur Scouting
Ron Sutter	Western Pro Scout
Tom Webster	Eastern Pro Scout
Scouts	Bob Atrill, Petti Hasanen, Tomas Jelinek, Larry Johnston, Sergei Samoylov, Al Tuer, Craig Demetrick, Fred Devereaux, Randy Hansch, Ralph Scmidt

MEDICAL & TRAINING STAFF
Morris Boyer	Athletic Therapist
Gerry Kurylowich	Assistant Athletic Therapist
Rich Hesketh	Strength & Conditioning Coach
Gus Thorson	Equipment Manager
Les Jarvis	Assistant Equipment Manager
Dr. Kelly Brett	Team Physician
Dr. Jim Thorne	Team Physician
Dr. Bill Blair	Team Dentist
Jules Carriere	Dressing Room Attendant
Dave Hamilton	Visiting Dressing Room Attendant

COMMUNICATIONS
Peter Hanlon	Director, Communications
Sean O'Brien	Manager, Media Relations
Bernie Hargrave	Administrative Assistant, Communications
Trevor Elgar	Community Relations Coordinator
Jim "Bearcat" Murray	Community Relations Ambassador

ADMINISTRATION
Hansine Ullberg	Director of Finance
Karen Kingham	Controller
Trudy McInnes	Assistant Controller
Kelly Shillington	Assistant Controller
Judy O'Brien	Executive Assistant to President & CEO
Judith Virag	Executive Assistant to Finance & Administration

MARKETING & SALES
Jim Bagshaw	Vice President, Advertising, Sponsorship, Marketing
Rollie Cyr	Vice President, Sales & Ticket Operations
Pat Halls	Senior Director, Sponsorship Sales
Kip Reghenas	Director, Retail FanAttic
Bob White	Director, Executive Suites
Kevin Gross	Business Development Manager
Mike Franco	Sales Manager
Dave Imbach	Director, Entertainment
Carlo Petrini	Director/Producer, Jumbotron
Laurie Wheeler	Publishing
Yvette Mutcheson	Executive Assistant to VP, Advertising, Sponsorship, Marketing
Harvey the Hound	Mascot

PENGROWTH SADDLEDOME
Libby Raine	VP, Building Operation
George Greenwood	Operations Manager
Art Hernandez	Food Services Manager
Sheila Parisien	Concessions Manager
Bob Godun	Security/Parking Manager

CALGARY HITMEN (WHL)
Kelly Kisio	General Manager
Blaine Forsythe	Assistant General Manager
Richard Kromm	Head Coach
Bruno Campese	Assistant Coach

LOWELL LOCK MONSTERS (AHL)
Elkin McCallum	Owner/Governor
Brian Martin	President
Ron Smith	Head Coach
Tom Rowe	Assistant Coach

Birth of the Calgary Flames

The Atlanta Flames came to life on June 6, 1972 when a group of businessmen, led by Tom Cousins, were granted a franchise into the NHL along with the New York Islanders. Selecting 2nd overall at that year's Amateur Draft, Atlanta made Jacques Richard the team's first selection after it had hired Cliff Fletcher away from the St. Louis Blues organization to act as the expansion team's first general manager.

The team chose the nickname "Flames" through a fan contest, the winning moniker appropriate to the region because General Sherman captured Atlanta during the Civil War and burned the city to the ground. Once the flames had been extinguished, Georgia's capital city was rebuilt.

The Flames improved in wins in each of the team's first four years, but playoff success was fleeting at best. The team played at The Omni in Atlanta, capacity 15,141, but it never established secure footing in the city the way that baseball's Braves and NFL's Falcons were a part of the city.

On May 21, 1980, Nelson Skalbania announced that he and a group of investors had purchased the team and were moving it to Alberta for the coming season. The team retained the Flames' nickname, but the burning "A" on the sweater became a "C" with more noticeable fiery flames shooting out the body of the letter. A year and a half later, Skalbania sold his interest in the team, leaving six men behind the ownership structure of the team.

Originally, the Calgary Flames played out of the tiny Stampede Corral (capacity 7,242) for three years until the Olympic Saddledome was completed in preparation for the 1988 Olympic Winter Games. Their first regular season NHL game occurred on October 9, 1980, a 5-5 tie against the Quebec Nordiques, and their last at the Corral, on April 18, 1983, was a 6-5 playoff win over provincial nemesis Edmonton.

The team's performance changed virtually overnight at its new home. From a sub-.500 record of 32-34-14 in '82-'83, the Flames reversed the wins and losses column to finish their first year the Saddledome with a 34-32-14 record, their first of nine successive seasons above .500. In the team's first game at the Saddledome, October 15,1983, the Flames defeated the Oilers 4-3. They got their first taste of greatness in 1986 when they went to the Stanley Cup Finals where the inexperienced team lost to Montreal in five games. Three years later, they got their revenge, becoming the first team in NHL history to win the Cup at the Montreal Forum, in a six-game series in which Doug Gilmour scored the Cup-winning goal in the third period of a 4-2 win.

Unexpectedly, it was to be the team's last series win for some 15 years. Along the way, the Flames added six new owners (on August 8, 1994) and saw two original owners, Norman Kwong and Sonia Scurfield, sell their interests in the team. In 2001, the ownership group bought out two of its number, Dr. Grant Bartlett and Ronald Joyce, and on August 29, 2003, the number of owners increased to eight when Clayton Riddell came on board.

Additionally, the Flames owners took control of the building on August 1, 1994, and soon after sold the naming rights to Canadian Airlines (starting in 1995-96) and later to Pengrowth (beginning in 2001-02), its current supporter.

To support the "Year of the Cowboy" celebrations in their city in 1998, the Flames unveiled a third sweater, a design that featured a horse's head with flames shooting out of its nostrils. Two years later, that sweater became the regular road version, and in the summer of 2003 the team returned to a new, red sweater and the black, horse's head sweater became the alternate model for select games only. The Flames' appearance in the 2004 Stanley Cup Finals marks the first Finals' placing for a Canadian team since Vancouver in 1994, when the Canucks lost a thrilling seven-game series to the New York Rangers.

Training Camp Roster and Player Movement

48 D Thomas Bellemare—returned to junior (Drummondville, QMJHL) on September 17

55 F Garrett Bembridge—returned to Lowell on September 22

15 F Blair Betts—NHL roster

17 F Chris Clark—NHL roster

2 D Mike Commodore—returned to Lowell prior to start of season

22 F Craig Conroy—NHL roster

53 F Cam Cunning—returned to junior (Kamloops, WHL) on September 17

41 F Matt Davidson—returned to Lowell on September 29

38 F Robert Dome—returned to Lowell on October 7

51 F Ryan Donally—returned to junior (Windsor, OHL) on September 17

16 F Shean Donovan—NHL roster

36 D Deryk Engelland—returned to Lowell on September 22

43 D Brennan Evans—returned to Lowell on September 22

58 F Jeff Ewasko—released outright on September 29

21 D Andrew Ference—NHL roster

3 D Denis Gauthier—NHL roster

23 F Martin Gelinas—NHL roster

26 F Josh Green—returned to Lowell on October 7

52 F Kevin Harvey—returned to junior (Owen Sound, OHL) on September 17

12 F Jarome Iginla—NHL roster

54 F Tyler Johnson—returned to junior (Moose Jaw, WHL) on September 17

7 F Chuck Kobasew—NHL roster

35 G Brent Krahn—returned to Lowell on October 7

4 D Jordan Leopold—NHL roster

Chris Simon celebrates his second-period goal in a game against Vancouver on April 11, 2004.

49	F	Matt Lombardi—NHL roster
10	F	Dave Lowry—NHL roster
32	D	Toni Lydman—NHL roster
68	F	Darren Lynch—returned to junior (Vancouver, WHL) on September 17
37	F	Dean McAmmond—NHL roster
33	G	Jamie McLennan—exposed in Waiver Draft, October 3, unclaimed
5	D	Steve Montador—NHL roster
46	F	Jason Morgan—returned to Lowell on September 29
33	F	Krzysztof Oliwa—NHL roster
30	D	Davis Parley—returned to Texas (ECHL) on September 29
42	D	Dion Phaneuf—returned to junior (Red Deer, WHL) on September 19
47	D	Tim Ramholt—returned to junior (Cape Breton, QMJHL) on September 17

28	D	Robyn Regehr—NHL roster
27	F	Steve Reinprecht—NHL roster
45	D	Roman Rozakov—returned to Lowell on September 29
50	G	Dany Sabourin—returned to Lowell on September 30
19	F	Oleg Saprykin—NHL roster
25	F	Martin Sonnenberg—returned to Lowell on September 22
56	F	Jamie Tardif—returned to junior (Peterborough, OHL) on September 17
1	G	Roman Turek—NHL roster
24	D	Jesse Wallin—returned to Lowell on October 7
44	D	Rhett Warrener—NHL roster
11	F	Stephane Yelle—NHL roster

The Regular Season

GAME 1

October 9, 2003
Calgary 1 at **Vancouver 4**

The Flames started their 2003-04 run to the Stanley Cup Finals with a pedestrian road game that did little to give the team momentum from day one. They allowed two power-play goals to the Canucks in the first period, but the home side was motivated by a moving pre-game tribute to the late Roger Neilson. Canucks alumni Richard Brodeur, Darcy Rota, Tiger Williams, and Doug Halward waved towels from their hockey sticks to recall Neilson's historic and popular antics during the 1982 Cup Finals. The Flames scored late in the second period when Chris Clark scooped a rebound to the left of goalie Daniel Cloutier to make it 2-1, but before the end of the period Jarkko Ruutu restored the Canucks' two-goal lead. "It's deflating," captain Jarome Iginla said afterward. "We were working hard, but anytime you can score a goal in the first or last five minutes of a period, there is a big emotional boost for the team that gets it." Iginla had been named team captain just two days earlier when Craig Conroy took off the "C" in the hopes that the talented former Art Ross Trophy winner would lead the team. Coach Brian Sutter agreed with Iginla's assessment. "It wasn't the difference in the game," he said of that third goal, "but it hurt any momentum we had built up." Sure enough, the Flames managed just five shots in the third and the Canucks scored the lone goal of the period, Jason King notching his first career goal midway through the final 20 minutes.

GAME 2

October 11, 2003
San Jose 2 at **Calgary 3**

The Flames won their home opener with a solid win but they lost their number-one goalie, Roman Turek, early in the second period on an Alyn McCauley goal that gave the Sharks a 2-1 lead. McCauley caught the Flames flat-footed on a bad line change and had a breakaway, but as he deked the goalie and scored he tumbled into Turek and caught the goalie's head with his knee. Both players were stunned, but McCauley eventually got up and Turek had to be helped off the ice. Jamie McLennan replaced him and kept the Sharks off the scoresheet the balance of the night. Stephane Yelle tied the game later in the second period, and in the third a Shean Donovan power-play goal early on proved to be the difference. Donovan hammered a hard slapshot past Evgeni Nabokov after a perfectly angled dump-in from Yelle, and the Flames played solid defence the rest of the way before 17,039 cheering fans. The Flames opened the scoring in the first after a beautiful move by Oleg Saprykin behind the net and a lovely pass out to Chuck Kobasew in front on the man advantage. Nils Ekman beat Turek with a wrist shot to tie the game near the end of the period, his first NHL goal in two and a half years. McLennan earned the victory for Calgary, his first in nearly a year during which time he had gone 0-10-3 in 18 appearances.

GAME 3

October 14, 2003
Edmonton 0 at **Calgary 1**

Jamie McLennan made his first start of the year with Roman Turek still on the sidelines with a head injury, and he promptly went out and stopped all 19 Edmonton shots to give the Flames their second consecutive win on home ice. This after a 2002-03 season in which they were the only team in the Western Conference to have a losing record at home. The lone goal of the game came on a

Vancouver goalie Dan Cloutier makes a save as Calgary's Dean McAmmond looks for a rebound during the season opener.

Oleg Saprykin watches the puck roll past goalie Tommy Salo for the game's only goal in Calgary's 1-0 win over Edmonton.

Calgary power play when Blair Betts drilled a hard shot between the pads of Tommy Salo with just one second left in Radek Dvorak's slashing penalty. It was a just result given that the team hit the goalpost twice in the first period, but the Oilers had some bad luck of their own. Ethan Moreau, Mike York, and Ryan Smyth all had excellent chances to tie the game, but McLennan was rock solid in the blue ice and extended his shutout streak to more than 97 minutes and kept his GAA for 2003-04 at 0.00 in the young season. Of note, this was the first victory for McLennan via a shutout in some three years, his previous two goalless games coming in 0-0 ties. By local standards, this was a restrained chapter in the often turbulent wars that are the Battle of Alberta, but the teams still played

five more times during the regular season and tensions were likely to heat up sooner rather than later.

GAME 4
October 18, 2003
Buffalo 2 at Calgary 0

Roman Turek was back in goal for the Flames, but he was unable to keep alive the shutout streak that had been started by his replacement, Jamie McLennan, as he surrendered two goals in a frustrating loss for the team. Chris Drury, erstwhile forward of the Flames now playing for the Sabres, returned to the Saddledome where he was booed lustily by the hometown fans. Less than two minutes into the game, however, he silenced his many Calgary critics by

setting up Ales Kotalik for the opening goal. The Flames thought they tied the game a short while later when Chuck Kobasew scored, but the referee ruled goalie interference and disallowed the first-period marker. The game's tone changed in the second period when Buffalo's Adam Mair was given a five-minute major and game misconduct for slashing Denis Gauthier, but the Flames generated few chances on the extended power play and the Sabres gained momentum from the kill. With less than one second left on the clock in the middle period, Miro Satan doubled the visitors' lead when he shoved the puck over the goal line on a mad scramble in front of Turek. In the third, the Sabres shut the door on Calgary, sending the 14,139 fans home grumpy.

GAME 5

October 21, 2003
Calgary 3 at Minnesota 2

Playing Minnesota was just the tonic Jarome Iginla needed. He had recorded 17 career points in 16 games against the Wild, but heading into the Flames' fifth game of the season he and linemates Craig Conroy and Dean McAmmond had failed to register a single point among them, and the team's five goals in those four games was dead last in the league. Enter coach Sutter, who moved "Iggy" onto a line with Matt Lombardi. The pair combined for two goals in the second period to erase a 1-0 Wild lead in the first, and the Flames went on to win their first road game of the year. Richard Park opened the scoring for Minnesota, but Iginla tied the game just 1:45 into the second period. Less than four minutes later, Lombardi gave the Flames a lead they never relinquished when he banked a shot in off the skate of goalie Dwayne Roloson. Chuck Kobasew gave the team a two-goal lead early in the third, and goalie Jamie McLennan, starting for Turek who was now sidelined with a knee injury, improved to 3-0-0 on the year.

GAME 6

October 24, 2003
St. Louis 2 at Calgary 1

Playing in their sixth road game of the seven games they've played and without four of their starting defencemen, the St. Louis Blues were ripe for defeat, but the low scoring Flames could not match their visitors' intensity and fell to 3-3-0 on the year with the 2-1 loss. The Blues put the Flames on their heels with an early power-play goal, Doug Weight backhanding the puck past Jamie McLennan to the side of the goal. Midway through the period Matt Lombardi tied the game, taking a nice pass from behind the goal by Steve Reinprecht and banking the shot off goalie Chris Osgood's skate and into the net to make it 1-1. Later in the period, Dean McAmmond was driven head first into the boards by Jeff Heerema and did not return, though the Blues forward was not penalized on the play. After a scoreless second period, the Blues went ahead for good when, ironically, Heerema capitalized on a Calgary miscue. Lombardi gave the puck up just inside his own blueline and Pavol Demitra fed Heerema a perfect pass from the corner that he one-timed past McLennan. The Flames were short-handed six times but had only one power play all night, leaving McLennan with a 3-1-0 record and the 15,454 fans disappointed by the team's fourth loss of the young season.

GAME 7

October 25, 2003
Calgary 4 at Edmonton 2

It was only four goals, not a deluge by any stretch, but it was a season high for the Flames in the early going of the young year, and it was the big guns who did most of the damage.

Minnesota's Alexandre Daigle makes an acrobatic pass while Calgary's Jordan Leopold looks on.

Calgary's Martin Gelinas is checked by Edmonton's Mike York during the Flames' 4-2 win in Edmonton.

Craig Conroy, Jarome Iginla, and Steve Reinprecht all scored, and Krzysztof Oliwa counted his first goal in almost three years and some 115 games to give the Flames their second win of the year against their provincial nemesis. Unlike game one, this was a bruising affair from the word go, the first period including some five fights and 70 penalty minutes. In fact, George Laraque and Oliwa were sent to the penalty box for fighting just two seconds after the opening faceoff. The only goal of the period came on a power play when Conroy scored his first of the season, one-timing a cross-ice pass from Steve Reinprecht. The Oilers took the lead 2-1 early in the second period when they scored two quick goals with the man advantage, but Iginla tied the game late in the period on a nice deflection off an Andrew Ference pass past Tommy Salo. In the third, the Flames scored two early goals of their own, and goalie Jamie McLennan closed the door to preserve the victory for the Flames, who won for the fourth time in seven starts.

GAME 8
October 28, 2003
Calgary 2 at **Colorado 4**

No team would have had much of a chance tonight, for it was the night that the Avalanche paid tribute to recently-retired goalie Patrick Roy. During the warm-up, every member of the Avs wore his number 33, and then Roy came out to centre ice to watch that same number raised to the rafters where it will remain ever-more. His team then skated to a quick 2-0 advantage courtesy of the power play. In the first instance, Jarome Iginla racked up 19 minutes in penalties and watched from the box as Milan Hejduk scored the game's first goal. A short time later, Adam Foote made it 2-0. The Flames didn't get on the board until early in the second when Chuck Kobasew roared down the right wing and timed a perfect pass in front that Martin Gelinas redirected past Roy's successor, the Swiss star David Aebischer. The Avs restored their two-goal lead before the end of the period, and a Kobasew-to-Gelinas combination early in the third on the power play brought the Flames to within a goal, but they got no closer. Rob Blake scored into the empty net with Jamie McLennan on the bench for an extra attacker.

Calgary goalie Dany Sabourin, in his first NHL game, makes a save during Dallas's 4-3 win over the visiting Flames.

the puck in, and a short time later Chuck Kobasew banked a shot in off goalie Marty Turco's skate. That spelled the end of the line for Turco, and the Flames entered the third period with a solid 3-1 lead. That lead disappeared thanks to Guerin. He scored on a power play, and on that same play he also took a penalty. Two minutes later, he raced out of the box, took a cross-ice pass from Arnott, and tied the game 3-3. In overtime, Arnott banged in a loose puck in the crease after Sabourin had made the initial save.

GAME 10
November 1, 2003
Columbus 0 at **Calgary 3**

The Flames snapped a two-game losing streak with a shutout victory thanks to the team's defence at both ends of the ice. In their own end, they limited the Blue Jackets to just 15 shots, all of which were stopped by Jamie McLennan, and on offense Jordan Leopold scored two first period goals to lead the attack. It was the first two-goal game for the Flames' defenceman, and it was the first goal for the team's blueline corps this season in their tenth game. The Flames were the last team in the NHL not to have a goal from their defencemen. Leopold scored both goals in a similar fashion, moving in off the point and sneaking behind his man to take a perfect pass and beat goalie Marc Denis. In the first instance, the pass came from Steve Reinprecht and Leopold shot high. In the second, it was Jarome Iginla who made the pass, and this time Leopold went five-hole with his shot. Shean Donovan added an empty netter late in the third to give the Flames a record of 5-4-0-1 and move into a tie for second place in the Northwest Division, behind the red-hot Vancouver Canucks. It was McLennan's second shutout of the year.

GAME 9
October 29, 2003
Calgary 3 at **Dallas 4**
(Arnott 0:17 OT)

The Flames extended a winless streak in Dallas that dated to December 2001 with a gutsy effort that fell just short, thanks to a three-goal performance by Bill Guerin of the Stars and a goal by Jason Arnott just 17 seconds into overtime. It was a game that saw the Flames start strong and finish weak, perhaps because they arrived in Texas in the wee hours after playing in Denver the previous night. Jarome Iginla scored midway through the first to give the visiting Flames a 1-0 lead, but Guerin tied the score when his backhander from in close beat Dany Sabourin, who was making his NHL debut. The Flames took control in the second period, scoring two goals of dubious character. First, Oleg Saprykin came out from behind the goal and poked

Darren McCarty beats Jamie McLennan in the second period of Detroit's 3-0 win in Calgary.

GAME 11

November 4, 2003
Detroit 3 at Calgary 0

The Flames were in trouble right when they knew Curtis Joseph would get the start for Detroit. The man they call Cujo improved his record to 24-8-3 lifetime against the Flames with his third shutout against Calgary, and the Flames lost for the third time in four games. This was not the same team that beat Columbus 3-0 a few days earlier. Brendan Shanahan broke out of his early-season slump, scoring his first two goals of the year in this his tenth game. He opened the scoring in the first minute of the second period, taking a pass from Mathieu Schneider on the power play and one-timing his patented, off-wing shot from the top of the left circle past Jamie McLennan. Just a few minutes later, Jarome Iginla turned the puck over in the centre-ice area and Darren McCarty walked in on a breakaway and put the Wings up 2-0 with a nifty goal. Coach Sutter put the rookie Dany Sabourin in the third period, not because of anything McLennan had done but instead to give the rookie a period's worth of play on home ice. Shanahan's second goal of the game, in the third, was the result of another turnover, this time by Oleg Saprykin, and a pretty three-way passing play saw Shanahan ice the victory for the visiting Wings.

GAME 12

November 7, 2003
Minnesota 3 at Calgary 0

Avenging a 3-2 loss at home to Calgary earlier in the year, the Minnesota Wild made the season a little more miserable for the Flames who were now without a goal for more than 122 minutes. They were shut out by the Wings by the same score three nights earlier, though this defeat was a little harder to swallow. Marc Chouinard scored the only goal of the first period when he converted a 2-on-1 with Alexandre Daigle, and midway through the second Richard Park scored his third goal of the season, a power-play marker that made it 2-0. Craig Conroy was guilty of a terrible giveaway in the third that led to the final Wild goal, by Pascal Dupuis, and despite outshooting Minnesota 18-5 in the final 20 minutes the Flames were booed off the ice by 13,839 disgruntled fans. The team now has just 21 goals in 12 games, dead last in the league, and has been shut out three times in eight home games. Calgary also sits in last place in the Northwest Division, out of a playoff spot.

GAME 13

November 9, 2003
Calgary 3 at **Columbus 4**

Coach Darryl Sutter always calls a spade a spade, and he had been quick through the early part of the year to credit goalie Jamie McLennan with being the team's best player to date. Tonight, he placed the blame for the team's third successive defeat squarely in the goalie's crease, saying, "we couldn't make a save in the second period, and it cost us the game." Perhaps, but taking bad penalties was a contributing factor to McLennan's misfortunes this evening, as the Blue Jackets went 3-for-8 on the power play while shutting out Calgary on five chances with the extra man. Surprisingly, it was tough guy Jody Shelley who counted twice for Columbus. He scored midway through the first to tie the game after Steve Reinprecht had given the Flames a lead just 2:41 after the opening faceoff. In the second, the Flames again took the lead, and again

Shelley scored to draw the score even, 2-2. But the Flames incurred six minor penalties in the middle period, and Columbus scored twice. It was the first of these, an Andrew Cassels goal, that had Sutter upset. He pulled McLennan and put young Dany Sabourin in the goal, though less than a minute later he, too, was victim of a Columbus power-play goal. Andrew Ference scored early in the third to make the game close, but although the Flames fired a season high 45 shots at Marc Denis in the Blue Jackets' goal, they could not get the equalizer and went down to defeat for the third time in a row.

GAME 14

November 12, 2003
Calgary 6 at Chicago 2

It was a Viking battle of coaches tonight as Darryl Sutter (Calgary) faced brother Brian (Chicago) for the first time this season. The Flames, who had scored just six goals in their

previous four games, matched that total in one night, an impressive showing led by rookie Matt Lombardi who had three goals and an assist in the win to break out of a seven-game goalless drought. Lombardi opened the scoring in the first at 8:10 on the power play when he banged in a rebound, then assisted on linemate Chris Clark's second goal of the year to make it 2-0. The Hawks scored before the end of the period, but Calgary took control of the game in the second, scoring three times in just over four minutes to build a solid 5-1 lead and chase starting goalie Michael Leighton from the nets. Dean McAmmond, a former Blackhawks forward, scored two of the goals and Lombardi had the other. He completed the hat trick by converting a short-handed breakaway in the third period, beating Craig Anderson, Leighton's replacement. The game was the second on a four-game road trip for the Flames and was played before just 11,988 fans in the Windy City.

Flames defenceman Denis Gauthier pushes future Flames forward Ville Nieminen of the Hawks into goalie Jamie McLennan.

Shean Donovan of the Flames is checked closely by a Nashville Predator during a 4-1 loss by the Flames on the road.

GAME 15

November 13, 2003
Calgary 1 at **Nashville 4**

With the Flames' fourth loss in five games, fans could rightly use the "S" word to describe their team. The Slump continued down in the Music City, and there was little in the way of positives to take from this encounter, the third of a four-game road trip for Calgary. Toni Lydman scored the first goal of the game, at 6:26 of the first, to give the Flames an early 1-0 lead, but it was all "Smashville" from there on. Marek Zidlicky tied the game in the final minute of the period, and in the second Vladimir Orszagh scored the only goal to give the Predators a lead they never relinquished. They added two more goals in the final 20 minutes, including one from David Legwand on a two-on-one break. Adam Hall closed out the

scoring, beating Dany Sabourin on a breakaway with two minutes to go. The game ended on a nasty note when goalie Tomas Vokoun chased Flames captain Jarome Iginla into the corner in the final minute, the resultant melee producing just three minor penalties but plenty of hard feelings.

GAME 16

November 15, 2003
Calgary 1 at **Edmonton 2**
(Smyth 4:44 OT)

Round three in the Battle of Alberta featured great goaltending from two backups, Calgary still using Jamie McLennan while Roman Turek convalesced and Ty Conklin in the nets with Tommy Salo still on the shelf. Nonetheless, it was an intense game without the fisticuffs, a game in which momentum changed through-

out the evening. Mike York got the game's first goal just 3:15 into the game when he deked McLennan on an odd-man rush. Calgary got its only goal in the second when rookie Matt Lombardi scored his sixth goal of the season late in the period on a quick wraparound that surprised Conklin. There was no scoring in the third, and both teams were perfect on the penalty kill, the Oilers going 0-for-4 with the man advantage, the Flames 0-for-5. Late in the overtime, though, Mike York tore down the right side while Smyth darted to the net. Despite the fact that forward Shean Donovan was all over him, Smyth touched his stick to the ice just as York fired a pass across, and the Oilers' captain redirected the puck past McLennan to give the Oilers a dramatic, last-minute victory. The loss left Calgary in 14th spot overall in the Western Conference.

GAME 17

November 18, 2003
Toronto 2 at **Calgary 3**
(Lydman 1:24 OT)

One of Toronto's homes away from home is Calgary, and many of the over-capacity crowd of 17,509 stuffed into the Pengrowth Saddledome on this Tuesday night saw their home side defeat the Leafs for just the third time in the past eleven tries in Calgary. Steve Reinprecht and Jarome Iginla each had a hand in all their team's goals. The Leafs entered the game in a slump during their six-game road trip, but they got off on the right foot when defenceman Bryan McCabe beat Jamie McLennan with a slap-shot that tipped off Dave Lowry's stick in front. But on a power play less than four minutes later, Iginla slid a nice backhand pass to Reinprecht in front and he managed to get the puck through goalie Ed Belfour to tie the game, 1-1. The Flames scored the only goal of the second, also on a power play, when Dean McAmmond roofed a loose puck in front. The final goal of regulation came early in the third when Toronto captain Mats Sundin snapped a quick shot that surprised McLennan. In the overtime, it was all Flames as they outshot the Leafs 5-0. The decisive play came when Iginla set up Reinprecht going to the net. Belfour made the sprawling save but he was in no position to stop Lydman who chipped the puck into the top of the net for the OT victory.

GAME 18

November 20, 2003
Montreal 1 at **Calgary 2**

If the Flames could identify a turning point early in the season, these back-to-back wins over Canada's two Original Six teams, Toronto and Montreal, would certainly be one obvious place. This win over the

The Flames' Robyn Regehr and Toronto's Owen Nolan mix it up along the boards during Calgary's critical 3-2 win over the Leafs.

Canadiens was perhaps even slightly larger in that it was the first start and win for goalie Miikka Kiprusoff whom the Flames had acquired a few days earlier to relieve the pressure on Jamie McLennan. Roman Turek's knee injury left him out of the lineup indefinitely, and Kiprusoff came in and stopped 22 of 23 Montreal shots. In fact, the only one he didn't stop was Craig Rivet's power-play goal late in the first period, a goal that gave his team a 1-0 lead. The Flames struck late, though, on a power play at 19:07 of the first, Steve Reinprecht being the marksman.

There was no scoring in the second, and as the third period wound down, overtime seemed inevitable. With less than two minutes to play, though, the Flames scored the winner off a faceoff, appropriate given that they dominated in the faceoff circle all night. On the winning play, Craig Conroy beat Saku Koivu on the draw. Koivu went 9-for-21 on the night, and this loss cost him most of all. Conroy got the puck back to Jordan Leopold at the point off a draw in the Montreal end and his quick shot was stopped by Jose Theodore. Martin Gelinas was right

Calgary's Oleg Saprykin and Chicago's Mark Bell get tangled up in front of Hawks' goalie Craig Anderson during the Flames' 2-1 victory.

there for the rebound, though, and he made no mistake from in close. The Flames held on for the victory and began a streak that saw them play in a way that anticipated their strong playoff run.

GAME 19

November 22, 2003
Chicago 1 at **Calgary 2**

The Flames won their third game in a row in dramatic fashion, Dean McAmmond scoring the game winner with less than a minute left in regulation time. It was the second win for the Flames against Chicago and moved the team back into the playoffs in the Western Conference. The Blackhawks were now winless in eight games. Steve Reinprecht scored first, on a second-period power play with Tuomo Ruutu in the penalty box for elbowing. The lead held up until 1:21 of the third when Kyle Calder scored his seventh goal of the year for the Hawks. McAmmond's winner came after he intercepted a clearing pass by defenceman Alexander

Karpovtsev along the boards and cut sharply in on goalie Craig Anderson. McAmmond slid the puck under the falling goalie at 19:11 to give the Flames the victory. Miikka Kiprusoff won his second straight game since joining the team, stopping 24 of 25 shots in the process.

GAME 20

November 27, 2003
Colorado 6 at Calgary 5
(Morris 2:24 OT)

The Colorado Avalanche stopped Calgary's three-game winning streak by scoring on the first shot of the game and the last shot, in overtime, in a contest that saw the lead change five times. The winning goal came on a nice pass from Alex Tanguay to Derek Morris, driving hard to the goal, as he took the puck in the slot and drilled a shot off the post to beat Miikka Kiprusoff at 2:24 of the extra period. Adam Foote scored just 1:02 into the game, but Shean Donovan and Oleg Saprykin scored midway through the period to give the Flames the lead. Donovan's was a short-handed goal on a breakaway as he deked David Aebischer and tucked the puck into the open side. Milan Hejduk tied the game 2-2 before the end of the period. The teams exchanged power-play goals in the second, Jordan Leopold giving the Flames a 3-2 lead before Joe Sakic tied the game again, but Teemu Selanne scored a short-handed goal at 17:10 to put the Avs up once again. Saprykin and Andrew Ference scored for the Flames in the third, but Travis Brigley notched Colorado's fifth goal between the two Calgary scores and the game went to overtime. Jarome Iginla had a great chance to win the game late in the third for the Flames, but he hit Aebischer square in the logo and remained goalless on home ice so far this season. The Flames' record is now 9-8-0-3.

GAME 21
November 29, 2003
Vancouver 4 at Calgary 4

With this 4-4 tie, the Flames continued their poor home showing against Vancouver, their record now 0-5-2 in the past seven games against the Canucks. It was a game that had some good and bad for the Flames, the good coming in their ability to rally from 3-1 down, the bad coming in their inability to hold a 4-3 lead late in the game. Brendan Morrison scored the only two goals of the first period, giving the Canucks a strong 2-0 lead, but Shean Donovan scored early in the second to get the 18,159 hometown fans back on their feet. Just 12 seconds later, though, rookie Ryan Kesler restored the two-goal advantage with his first career NHL goal, and then the Flames rallied. Robyn Regehr and Donovan scored just 40 seconds apart to tie the game. Then, midway through the third period, Stephane Yelle scored his first goal in 14 games, on a power play, to give the Flames their first lead of the game. Morrison completed the hat trick at 17:51 when he got to a loose puck in the slot before Calgary goalie Jamie McLennan could find it. He made no mistake in sending it past the goalie to tie the game for the Canucks. The Flames dominated the overtime, but the game ended in a 4-4 tie.

GAME 22
December 2, 2003
San Jose 1 at **Calgary 3**

Shean Donovan had just five goals all of 2002-03, but his sixth goal of this new year was his most dramatic yet, a game winner in the second period on a penalty shot. Sharks defenceman Scott Hannan dragged Donovan down on a breakaway, and on the free shot the Flames' forward deked Vesa Toskala, and, moving left, slid the puck under the Sharks' goalie. The goal came at 19:06 of the second period and broke a 1-1 tie. It was all the team needed to complete an impressive six-game homestand with a record of 4-0-1-1. The goal also tied Donovan for the team lead with rookie Matt Lombardi. Jarome Iginla scored the first goal of the game earlier in the middle period, his first goal on home ice this season, on a breakaway, and his first score anywhere in almost a month. In the third he collected an assist on Martin Gelinas' empty-net goal to finish the scoring. This marked the first time new Flames goalie Miikka Kiprusoff faced his old team, San Jose, and the goalie who took the starter's job away from him, Toskala. It gave Kiprusoff a 3-1-0 record with the Flames. The win ended San Jose's five-game winning streak and put the Flames two games over .500 for the first time this season.

GAME 23
December 4, 2003
Calgary 4 at Vancouver 1

The Flames' train kept on a-rollin' out west as Calgary extended its undefeated string to seven games

Stephane Yelle (right) and Dean McAmmond (centre) congratulate Shean Donovan on a goal.

from the left faceoff circle eluded Dan Cloutier in the Canucks' goal, and midway through the second period Donovan made it 2-0 with a great wrist shot to the far corner. Martin Gelinas put the game out of reach in the first minute of the third, chasing down a loose puck in the corner and fooling Cloutier with a shot the goalie might normally have stopped. Trevor Linden broke Kiprusoff's shutout a short time later, but the Flames played poised hockey and never looked threatened.

GAME 24
December 5, 2003
Minnesota 1 at **Calgary 2**

The Iggy Express returned home to the Pengrowth Saddledome and the Flames extended their unbeaten streak to eight games (6-0-1-1) and improved to 12-8-1-3 on the season. Captain Jarome Iginla scored the game-winning goal with 22.8 seconds left in regulation time, his 8th goal of the year. Teammate Oleg Saprykin breezed into the Minnesota end after a bad line change by the Wild, and Manny Fernandez stopped his hard slapshot. The goalie couldn't control the rebound, however, and the puck landed at Iginla's skates and he tucked in the rebound to break a 1-1 tie. The Wild had scored the only goal of the first two periods, Pascal Dupuis doing the honours in the first period just 1:54 into the game on a rebound of his own. His team had to be feeling confident entering the third with a 1-0 lead, because the Wild had not lost a game while leading after two since March 5, 2002, a span of 47 games. But the red hot Flames answered just 1:43 into the third when Shean Donovan scored for the fifth time in six games, scoring a great goal on a backhand from in close as he was being taken to the ice by Darby Hendrickson.

Goalie Miikka Kiprusoff, still sporting his plain white mask, makes a save while defenceman Jordan Leopold ties up Vancouver's Jason King.

(5-0-1-1) with an impressive 4-1 win over the Canucks, division leaders in the Northwest. Not surprisingly, the team's charge matched the improved play of team captain Jarome Iginla, who had two goals this night, giving him ten points in his last seven games. Shean Donovan also continued his scoring ways, registering his fifth goal in the past four games, and goalie Miikka Kiprusoff was front and centre, stopping all but one of 29 shots he faced. Iginla scored the game's opening goal when his shot

GAME 25

December 7, 2003
Pittsburgh 1 at **Calgary 6**

Outscored 36-11 in first periods so far this year, the Pittsburgh Penguins could not fare any better this night against the streaking Flames, going to the dressing room down 3-1 to the home team after 20 minutes. Jordan Leopold scored just one minute into the game to give the Flames a lead, but Milan Kraft scored less than two minutes later to tie the game, 1-1. After Donovan scored his 9th goal of the season and extended his scoring streak to six straight games, though, the game was virtually over.

more insurance goals in the third as the Flames extended their unbeaten streak to five games and their home record to 9-4-1-1. Goalie Miikka Kiprusoff faced only 22 shots while at the other end Sebastien Caron was peppered with 43 shots. The 15,009 Flames' fans went home happy.

GAME 26

December 9, 2003
Calgary 1 at **Minnesota 2**

The Flames' five-game unbeaten streak was over, but it wasn't for lack of effort against a frustrating opponent. The Flames outshot Minnesota

goals. Unlike the last time these two teams met, when the Flames came back in the third period, the Wild played with greater defensive purpose and executed the trap to perfection. The only blemish on Manny Fernandez's record tonight was a late goal by Martin Gelinas, who was playing in his 1,000thNHL game. His goal at 15:28 gave the Flames some life, and a late power play added to their chances. Coach Sutter pulled Miikka Kiprusoff in the final minute, but the Flames couldn't muster too many great chances playing 6-on-4 and the Wild hung on for the win. It was just the second loss for Kiprusoff since joining the Flames eight games ago.

GAME 27

December 11, 2003
Carolina 0 at **Calgary 1**

Shean Donovan was having the kind of season a player hopes will continue. He scored his team-best 12th goal of the year early in the third period to give the Flames their fourth straight win at the Pengrowth Saddledome, and Miikka Kiprusoff stopped all 22 shots he faced for his fourth career shutout. Donovan was going to the bench when he saw defenceman Robyn Regehr control the puck and move up ice. He decided to join the rush, and although Kevin Weekes stopped Regehr's hard shot, he couldn't control the rebound. Donovan drove to the net, beating Hurricanes defenceman Sean Hill to the puck, and he chipped the puck over Weekes's shoulder while falling down. It was a goal created by driving to the net, and it gave the Flames an 8-1-1-2 record in their last 12 games. Kiprusoff faced only ten shots over the first 40 minutes but earned kudos for his play in the third when he faced a dozen shots and made a number of fine saves, notably a glove grab on Niclas Wallin and later Eric Staal.

Flames forward Oleg Saprykin is stopped by Sebastien Caron in the Penguins goal, but Calgary still managed an easy 6-1 victory.

Stephane Yelle scored the final goal of the first, and Oleg Saprykin added one in the second to extend the Calgary lead to 4-1. Donovan completed his first hat trick in three years with two

14-9 in the opening period, but the teams headed to the dressing room tied 0-0 after one. In the second, the Wild scored twice, Andrei Zyuzin and Pascal Dupuis counting the

GAME 28

December 13, 2003
Colorado 1 at Calgary 1

In days gone by, a 1-1 tie with the mighty Avalanche would feel like a win for the Flames, but in the dressing room after the game the players felt like they had lost the game because they deserved to win it. They did, indeed, deserve a better fate, but in extending their unbeaten streak at home to six games (4-0-2) they were victim to hot goaltending from David Aebischer in the Colorado net. The Avs had the best two chances to score in a goalless first period. Teemu Selanne drew goalie Miikka Kiprusoff out of the net, but when he released a shot, defenceman Denis Gauthier was there to fill the breach. Moments later, Andrei Nikolishin hit the post, and it was the Flames who drew first blood, early in the second period. Deam McAmmond tied Joe Sakic up on a faceoff in the Colorado end and linemate Shean Donovan knocked the puck back to defenceman Robyn Regehr at the point. His quick wrist shot fooled Aebischer, and the Flames had the better of the play for much of the rest of the game. It wasn't until midway through the third period that Colorado tied the game. Selanne came out from behind the goal and tried a wraparound, but the puck hit teammate Joe Sakic's skate and went right onto the stick of rookie John-Michael Liles who scored into the open side before Kiprusoff could move across the crease. In the overtime, the Avs had the better of the play, but Jarome Iginla had the best chance to score, whipping a shot off the post that had Aebischer clearly beaten. With the tie, the Avs extended their unbeaten streak to eight games (4-0-4).

Flames' defenceman Andrew Ference (left) and Colorado forward Dan Hinote collide during the teams' 1-1 tie in Calgary.

The ever-acrobatic Miikka Kiprusoff shows his flexibility and reach during Calgary's 3-2 win in Philadelphia.

GAME 29

December 16, 2003
Calgary 3 at Philadelphia 2
(McAmmond 3:33 OT)

Just as the Flames' back-to-back wins over Toronto and Montreal got the team on the right track, this win on the road against the Flyers proved they could play with the big boys. Philadelphia was ranked first overall in the NHL with 44 points, and the team's 12-1-2 record at the Wachovia Center reflected its dominance at home. To make matters worse for

Calgary, there was a buzz in Philadelphia this day as the Flyers had just acquired forward Mike Comrie from the Oilers, adding another 30-goal scorer to their already potent offence. No matter to the Flames. They got on the scoreboard first when Krzysztof Oliwa stole the puck inside the Flyers' zone and passed it to Jarome Iginla who rifled a shot past Jeff Hackett in the Philadelphia net at 2:31 of the opening period. Jeremy Roenick tied the game late in the first when he stepped over the blueline and blasted

a terrific slapshot past Miikka Kiprusoff. The home side went ahead in the second when John LeClair tipped a Joni Pitkanen slapshot on a power play. Undaunted, the Flames rallied again from a deficit after two periods, Dean McAmmond scooping in a loose puck during a mad scramble midway through the third. Kiprusoff made perhaps his best save in the overtime off a shot from defenceman Kim Johnsson to keep the score 2-2, and then McAmmond and Chuck Kobasew had a 2-on-1 with only defenceman Eric Weinrich back. Weinrich took away the pass, so McAmmond fired a high shot that eluded Hackett, and the Flames earned the extra point in the standings with the dramatic OT win.

GAME 30

December 18, 2003
Calgary 5 at Boston 0

Jamie McLennan got the start for Calgary tonight, giving Miikka Kiprusoff a night off, and his teammates helped him out by scoring on almost all of their good chances. A hot Flames team combined with a Bruins team with a weak home record produced this score before just 10,659 fans in Beantown. The Flames got first-period goals from Jarome Iginla and Josh Green on just four total shots, and led 2-0 after one period. In the second, they pulled away by scoring three goals in under six minutes, building a 5-0 lead with just nine shots on goal to that point. Jarome Iginla scored his 10th and 11th goals of the season, and McLennan stopped all 30 shots. The Flames managed just 14 shots at Andrew Raycroft and Felix Potvin, who took over for the starter at the beginning of the third period. The Flames are now 7-1-2-1 in their past eleven games and with the win moved into a tie for second place in the Northwest Division with Colorado.

GAME 31

December 19, 2003
Calgary 2 at Columbus 1

In the bizarre and wacky world of hockey, this game ranks right up there for a number of reasons. Columbus set a franchise record by having an extraordinary 13 power-play chances on the night, but not only did the Blue Jackets fail to score even once, they actually allowed a Calgary short-handed goal in the first period which turned out to be the game winner! And, in a first period in which the Jackets outshot the Flames 20-4, they went to the dressing room trailing 2-0! Martin Gelinas scored the game's first goal at 10:55 when he tipped a Jordan Leopold shot that squirted through Marc Denis and just over the goal line as he dove back in futile desperation to make the save. Then, later in the period, with Dean McAmmond in the penalty box for goaltender interference, Jarome Iginla and Matt Lombardi broke out on a 2-on-1. Iginla waited for Denis to come out and challenge him, and the Calgary captain slid the puck over to the rookie who redirected the puck in for his 7th goal of the season. That was all the Flames needed. Rick Nash scored the lone Columbus goal on a beautiful deke in the third period to ruin Miikka Kiprusoff's shutout. Late in the game Iginla scored again but video review ruled that the net was off its moorings when the puck crossed the line. The Flames moved into fifth spot overall in the Western Conference with 39 points and second place in the Northwest Division ahead of Colorado, which lost 1-0 to Anaheim this night.

GAME 32

December 23, 2003
Edmonton 1 at **Calgary 2**

Although this was a classic Battle of Alberta game on the night before Christmas Eve, these were two teams heading very much in opposite directions. With the win, the Flames now sported a record of 12-1-2-2 in their past 17 games and stretched their unbeaten streak at home to seven games (5-0-2), while the Oilers slipped to 2-9-4 in their past 15. Miikka Kiprusoff was the difference again for Calgary as he lowered his league-best average to 1.44 and improved his record with the Flames to 10-2-1. Calgary scored first, on the power play, in the opening period, taking advantage of Edmonton's weak penalty killing, the worst in the league. Oleg Saprykin knocked in a loose puck that Tommy Salo couldn't smother. In the second period, Matt Lombardi drove to the net, and although Salo swept the puck away it landed near Rhett Warrener and he popped the puck into the open side of the net to make the lead 2-0. It was his first goal in exactly 100 games. The Oilers got their game going in the third, but it was too little, too late. They counted a goal when Mike York knocked in a rebound off a Radek Dvorak shot, at 16:44, but although they controlled play for the last three minutes, they couldn't get the equalizer.

Goalie Miikka Kiprusoff makes the save while Columbus's Nikolai Zherdev looks for the rebound.

GAME 33

December 26, 2003
Vancouver 2 at Calgary 0

The Vancouver Canucks continued their mastery of the Flames right in Calgary, extending their unbeaten streak to eight games at the Saddledome (6-0-2) thanks to some timely scoring, a little bit of luck, and a sluggish Flames team. It was the first game for both teams after the Christmas break, and the visitors had the jump, skating to a 2-0 lead after the first period. Mattias Ohlund scored on a power play just 1:35 into the game with Martin Gelinas in the penalty box for high sticking, and Brendan Morrison doubled the lead later in the period. The Flames outshot the Canucks 15-6 in the second but came away empty-handed, and their best chance of the game didn't even count as a shot on goal. During fierce pressure in the Canucks crease early in the third period, Ohlund closed his hand on the puck and the Flames were awarded a penalty shot. Oleg Saprykin went in on goal and looked up and saw goalie Dan Cloutier well out of his net. Saprykin opted to shoot, and went wide with the chance, and Cloutier stopped everything else he faced to record his second shutout in three games. The game was the proverbial four-pointer, and with the win Vancouver extended its lead on Calgary for top spot in the division to five points.

GAME 34

December 28, 2003
Calgary 2 at Edmonton 1

For the fourth time in five games this year, the Battle of Alberta went to the Flames, and with this loss the Oilers' slump continued. They were now just 1-4-1 in their past six games. It was a quiet game by Alberta standards, the Flames building a 2-0 lead by the midway point of the third period before the Oilers got their only goal

Vancouver's Henrik Sedin hauls down Oleg Saprykin during a 2-0 win by the Canucks in this Boxing Day match in Calgary.

of the night. Dean McAmmond started the scoring with a beautiful one-timer off a cross-ice pass from Jarome Iginla, beating Tommy Salo with two minutes left in the second. Iginla then scored his 12th goal of the year in the third when he eluded defenceman Jason Smith, tore down the right wing, and powered a slapshot past Salo. Miikka Kiprusoff made his best stop of the night early in the third when he stopped Ryan Smyth on a short-handed breakaway, but Edmonton scored at 14:54 on a power play when Mike York banged in a rebound off his own shot.

GAME 35

December 29, 2003
Minnesota 2 at Calgary 2

Richard Park beat Calgary goalie Miikka Kiprusoff on a penalty shot in the third period to give Minnesota a fortunate 2-2 tie with the Flames at the Pengrowth Saddledome. In a game in which the Flames outshot their opponents 46-19, the goaltending of Dwayne Roloson in the Wild net proved to be the difference between a tie and a loss for the visitors. Pascal Dupuis opened the scoring at 16:46 of the first, knock-

ing home a loose puck after a shot by Sergei Zholtok. Despite getting 17 shots in that period, the Flames went to the dressing room trailing 1-0. They refused to give up, though, and in the second the shots were a lopsided 14-1 for the Flames, and they were rewarded with two goals, albeit fortunate ones at that. Martin Gelinas drove to the net and stopped suddenly, and in one motion threw the puck to the front of the net. It hit Zholtok in the backside and went past a stunned Roloson who had no chance on the play. Two minutes later, Dave Lowry carried the puck in over the line on a 2-on-1 with Chuck Kobasew, Andrei Zyuzin the lone defenceman back on the play. Lowry tried to make a pass across, but Zyuzin deflected the puck into his own goal while trying to prevent the cross-ice pass. Park's penalty shot came after defenceman Jordan Leopold relieved pressure in Kiprusoff's crease by picking the puck up and throwing it away. On the shot, Park made a slight move to freeze Kiprusoff and then roofed a backhander to tie the game, 2-2. The overtime settled nothing, and the Wild happily left the arena with a road point.

Former Calgary Flames defenceman Derek Morris plays the body against Chuck Kobasew during Colorado's 2-1 win over the Flames.

GAME 36

December 31, 2003
Colorado 2 at Calgary 1

In a playoff-type game, the Avalanche got goals from two less-heralded players and with their 2-1 win moved into a tie with the Flames for second spot in the Northwest Division. Peter Worrell made a nice deflection of a John-Michael Liles shot 8:10 into the first period to open the scoring, and then rookie Steve Moore converted a Dan Hinote pass in the slot by making a nice move and sliding the puck between the pads of Jamie McLennan. McLennan was starting for the injured Miikka Kiprusoff who had to leave the previous game in the first period with a sprained knee that will keep him out for four to six weeks. It was Moore's first career NHL goal in his 36th game. The Flames got their only goal in the second period when Rhett Warrener scored on a wrist shot off the post from the slot during a Calgary power play. Although the Flames took it to the Avs in the third, they couldn't get the equalizer and Colorado extended its unbeaten streak in Calgary to seven games (4-0-3).

GAME 37

January 3, 2004
Vancouver 3 at Calgary 1

Jarome Iginla's impact on the outcome of this game was great, but unlike the usual case where the superstar contributes goals and assists, this time it was two big misses on breakaways that helped the Canucks forge a 3-1 victory at the Pengrowth Saddledome. In the final minute of the first period, Iginla was hauled down by Brent Sopel on a clear-cut breakaway and was awarded a penalty shot, but with the free chance he lost control of the puck and didn't even test rookie Alex Auld with a shot. Vancouver scored at 6:04 of the second period to open the scoring, Markus Naslund counting his 20th goal of the season. Goalie Jamie McLennan mishandled a shoot-in and tipped the puck directly in front of his own goal while he was behind the net, and Naslund was right there to steer the puck into the open net. A few minutes later, the Canucks went on the power play, and that's when Iginla broke away with only the goalie to beat. Again, though, he muffed the play, shooting high over the glass and keeping the score 1-0 Vancouver. The Canucks added two goals later in the period to go up 3-0 after 40 minutes, and although Chris Clark got the Flames on the scoreboard early in the third, it wasn't enough to get the team a point.

GAME 38

January 5, 2004
Calgary 5 at Rangers 0

As a matchup of payrolls, this was David vs. Goliath if ever there was such a game in the NHL, and David hammered the big man with a 5-0 shellacking that gave the Flames their fifth straight win on the road. They are now 9-5-0-2 away from the Saddledome this season. Jarome Iginla led the attack with a goal and two assists, as did Andrew Ference who had two scores and a helper. Iginla's two goals were his 10th and 11th on the road of his 13 total this season. The first came at 6:48 when he blasted a shot past starter Jussi Markkanen in the Rangers' goal, and a few minutes later he was credited with a second goal when Andrew Ference's shot seemed to hit Iginla and go in. Scorekeepers later gave credit to Ference for the original shot. Matt Lombardi completed an overpowering first period for Calgary when he scored in the final minute to send the Flames to the dressing room up 3-0. Mike Dunham was in goal for the Rangers to start the second, but that goaltending change failed to kick-start the team's offence. Denis Gauthier scored the lone goal of the second, and then Ference scored his second of the game to ice the victory. He shot the puck into the Rangers

Flames defenceman Denis Gauthier blocks a shot from the Rangers' Alexei Kovalev during Calgary's easy 5-0 win on Broadway.

Jarome Iginla unleashes a slapshot before the Islanders' Michael Peca can stop him. The Flames won 3-2 on Long Island.

end along the glass, but as Dunham went behind the net to play the puck it hit a support and caromed directly into the net. That's how the game went for the Rangers. The win ended Calgary's three-game winless streak.

GAME 39
January 6, 2004
Calgary 3 at Islanders 2

Jarome Iginla proved once again why the Calgary Flames named him captain prior to the start of the season, why his performance is tied to the team's, why he is their highest-paid player. Iginla had two goals and an assist, giving him six points in two nights against the two New York teams. He scored the only goal of the first period in Long Island on a bit of a lucky play. Dave Lowry centred the puck to him, and goalie Garth Snow made the save. In the process, though, he kicked the puck out to Iginla and it hit him and went into the net. In the second, the Flames outshot the Islanders 19-8, but it was the home side that scored the first two goals of the period. Mattias Weinhandl and young sensation Jason Blake scored from in close, but Iginla led the comeback charge just a short time later. Oleg Saprykin redirected a wrist shot from Iginla past Snow, and then "Iggy" drilled a hard shot off the post and in on a Calgary power play to send the Flames to the second intermission with a 3-2 lead. In the third, goalie Jamie McLennan closed the door to keep the Flames' unbeaten streak alive. The last time they lost in Uniondale was back in December 1996. The win gave the Flames a record of 21-12-3-3 and kept them solidly in the playoffs in the Western Conference.

GAME 40
January 8, 2004
Calgary 1 at **Chicago 3**

In an 82-game schedule, every team has some off nights, and for the Flames this was one such evening. The Hawks had a record of just 4-16- 4-4 in their previous 24 games and were ripe for the picking, but Calgary simply couldn't muster the effort tonight despite scoring the game's first goal. On a power play early in the first, Robyn Regehr took a shot from the point that pinballed off a number of players, Oleg Saprykin being the last, and caromed past Michael Leighton and in. The lead didn't last to intermission, though, as Kyle Calder scored on a nice effort while being checked by Flames' defenceman Toni Lydman. The game's turning point came toward the end of the second period when Calgary had a four-minute power play and a two-man advantage for two full minutes. The team managed only one shot on goal – although Jordan Leopold hit the post – and as a result it was the Hawks that started the third with momentum. Steve Sullivan scored the game winner early in the final period on a Hawks power play, swatting the puck barely over the goal line on a mad scramble in front. Bryan Berard put the game on ice with a last minute empty netter.

GAME 41

January 10, 2004
Florida 2 at **Calgary 4**

Many good things came out of the Flames' home win after three games on the road. They reached the halfway point of the season by recording their 50th point in the standings, and they were led once again by captain Jarome Iginla, who had his third, three-point night in his past four games. Tonight it was two goals and an assist, and he helped ignite another rally that saw the Flames overcome a deficit heading into the third period. Nathan Horton opened the scoring with a power-play goal early in the first, but Iginla tied the game 1-1 when he knocked in a rebound from a Lynn Loyns shot while the Flames were short-handed. Kristian Huselius gave the visiting Panthers a 2-1 lead when he beat McLennan with a shot in a one-on-one situation, and there was no scoring in the second, a period in which the Flames took the game to Florida. In the first minute of the third, Iginla took a rising slapshot that goalie Roberto Luongo stopped, but the goalie couldn't control the rebound and Dean McAmmond scooped the loose puck into the net to tie the score, 2-2. Less than five minutes later, Chris Clark scored the go-ahead goal, and Iginla added insurance midway through the period. The three unanswered goals in the final period gave the Flames 22 wins in the first half of the season; they had 29 all of the 2002-03 schedule.

GAME 42

January 13, 2004
Calgary 1 at **Toronto 4**

After accumulating 50 points in the first 41 games of their schedule, the Flames merely flickered at the Air Canada Centre to kick of the second half of the season. In dropping a 4-1 decision to Toronto, Calgary man-

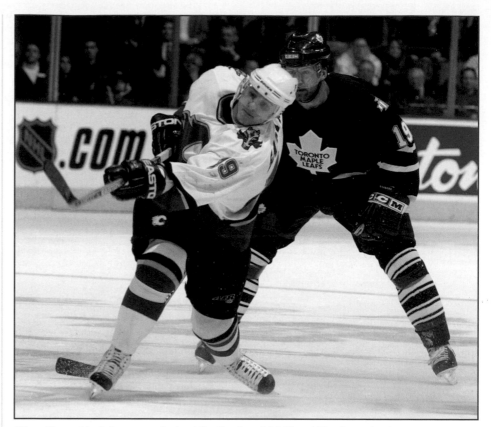

Oleg Saprykin lets go a shot while the Leafs' Mikael Renberg looks on.

aged only 16 shots and never seriously threatened Ed Belfour for any prolonged stretch. The Flames entered the game with the NHL's second best defensive record but were short on manpower with Craig Conroy, Dave Lowry, Chuck Kobasew, Miikka Kiprusoff, and Roman Turek all nursing injuries. Dany Sabourin was in uniform as Jamie McLennan's back up. However, the Maple Leafs were without Alexander Mogilny, Owen Nolan, Robert Reichel, and Tomas Kaberle. Prior to the game, Toronto's Tom Fitzgerald and former Calgary star Gary Roberts were honoured after reaching the 1,000-game milestone. Jarome Iginla presented Roberts with a limited edition print on behalf of the Flames. Jamie McLennan held his own in goal but his teammates were lacklustre in front of him. At one point he lost his blocker for 20 seconds but fortunately was not forced to make a save. The most noteworthy statistic was Krzysztof Oliwa building his NHL lead with his 18th

fighting major after tangling with Nathan Perrot. Shean Donovan scored the Flames' only goal by cutting around Toronto rookie blueliner Pierre Hedin and snapping a quick shot over Belfour's glove.

GAME 43

January 14, 2004
Calgary 3 at Washington 3

The Flames peppered Washington goalie Olaf Kolzig with 44 shots but settled for a tie in a very odd game. All six goals were scored in the final 5:37 of the third period. Washington coach Glen Hanlon noted, "It felt like a pee-wee game at the end – with all due respect to pee-wees." Jarome Iginla put the visitors in position for a win when he scored at 19:00 of the final frame. The party was ruined by a combination of wizardry and luck by Jaromir Jagr. The enigmatic forward scored on a near-impossible shot with 0.8 seconds left in regulation time. He was positioned behind the goal line when he desperately sent the puck toward the net. It bounced up off the bottom of the net then struck the back of Jamie McLennan's knee on the way down before crossing over the line to give the Capitals an improbable point. Most of the goals in this game were a result of odd bounces or mad scrambles in front of the goal. On one occasion, the Caps' Joel Kwiatowski knocked the puck into his own net and Matthew Lombardi was credited with his 9th goal of the year. Rather than sulk after Jagr's fluke, the Flames kept up the pressure by out shooting Washington 7-2 in overtime, but Kolzig was sharp. Calgary enjoyed a power play and a short 5-on-3 advantage but could not capitalize. Any frustration caused by this game was compounded by the loss of Stephane Yelle for a few weeks with a sprained MCL in his right knee.

GAME 44

January 17, 2004
Dallas 3 at Calgary 2

The Flames gave up third period goals to Jere Lehtinen and Jason Arnott to drop a 3-2 decision to Dallas. Of greater concern was the loss of Jarome Iginla with a leg injury late in the second period. Iginla battled Stars' defenseman Richard Matvichuk while trying to prevent an icing and was sent feet first into the end boards. This was supposed to be an upbeat night for the club as Roman Turek started in goal for the first time since tearing his MCL the first week of the regular season. In addition, hard working centre Craig Conroy was back in uniform after missing 19 games with a knee problem of his own. Conroy was reunited on a line with Martin

Gelinas and Shean Donovan, which had been the club's most effective trio prior to the injury. Calgary's first goal came with two seconds left on a two-man advantage. Steve Reinprecht faked going behind the net and slid a nifty pass to Chris Clark who one-timed a shot past Marty Turco. The Flames took the lead in the second period when Martin Gelinas deflected Shean Donovan's shot between Turco's pads. Despite the loss the club was relieved when X-rays and an MRI revealed no structural damage and that Iginla was only dealing with a mildly sprained ankle. The loss dropped Calgary to seventh place in the Western Conference behind the Nashville Predators.

Washington goalie Olaf Kolzig gets his blocker arm on Oleg Saprykin's shot during a 3-3 tie between the Capitals and Flames.

GAME 45
January 19, 2004
Calgary 5 at Anaheim 1

The Flames topped the Mighty Ducks 5-1 to claim their first win in Anaheim since January 13, 1999 to end a 0-6-3 skid in the L.A. suburb. They also played their first game of the season without captain Jarome Iginla who hurt his ankle in the previous game. Playing in his place, Chuck Kobasew registered a couple of assists while playing a robust game. Roman Turek kept his club in the game during the first period by limiting Anaheim to only one goal despite the Ducks' holding a 20-6 advantage in shots. The opening period was also marred by Krzysztof Oliwa's five-minute match penalty after he elbowed goalie Jean-Sebastien Giguere. The Flames killed off the five-minute major but gave up a goal after Turek inadvertently steered in Sergei Fedorov's pass across the crease. Calgary showed more jump in the second frame with three goals including tallies by Martin Gelinas and Oleg Saprykin only 2:14 apart which gave the Flames a 3-1 edge heading to the third. Gelinas' goal seemed to deflate the Ducks as he outworked their defense to force the puck under the pads of Giguere. Saprykin's goal was particularly frustrating for Anaheim as it went in off defenders Todd Simpson and Ruslan Salei. Goals by Josh Green and Chris Clark secured the win and Craig Conroy recorded a career-best four assists.

GAME 46
January 20, 2004
Calgary 1 at **Los Angeles 4**

The return of Jarome Iginla to the lineup did not spark the Flames as they put in an inferior effort in L.A. The Kings scored three first-period goals on broken coverage by Calgary's defense, which ran around, and left the slot unprotected. After falling behind 2-0, Calgary replaced Roman Turek with Jamie McLennan but the team remained in a funk the rest of the way. The Flames were victimized twice by rugged forward Ian Laperriere who broke out of a 29-game scoring slump in style. The Calgary netminders faced 35 shots and at the end of the second period the count stood 32-14 in favour of Los Angeles. Dean McAmmond, who notched his first short-handed effort in 622 career games, scored Calgary's only goal. It was a 50-foot shot from just inside the blueline that Roman Cechmanek probably wished he could have another chance at stopping. After the game, Calgary coach Darryl Sutter singled out weak goaltending and some sloppy play from Andrew Ference as the reasons for the loss. Krzysztof Oliwa sat out the game as a healthy scratch though he was still awaiting word on whether any disciplinary action was forthcoming after the incident with Jean-Sebastien Giguere the previous night.

GAME 47
January 22, 2004
Nashville 0 at **Calgary 4**

The Flames recovered from the loss in L.A. by winning most of the little battles and races for the puck against Nashville. They dealt the Predators their first loss in seven games in this penalty-filled contest. Roman Turek stopped 23 shots to record his 25th career shutout. It was Turek's fourth consecutive start after returning from his knee injury. Shean Donovan and Matthew Lombardi scored two goals each to pace Calgary. After scoring ten goals in eight games, Donovan scored just once in the next 19 before putting a pair behind the Predators' Tomas Vokoun. Lombardi broke out of a slump of his own as he had found the back of the net only three times in the previous 30 games. Both Lombardi and Donovan scored on the power play four minutes apart in the first period. Donovan's second goal of the game was also his second

Andrew Ference of Calgary (left) battles along the boards with Trent Klatt of L.A. during the Kings' 4-1 win over the Flames.

Oleg Saprykin tries unsuccessfully to score on Tampa Bay's backup goalie John Grahame. Who would have guessed that this game was a Stanley Cup preview?

short-handed marker of the season as he caught Vokoun by surprise with a shot that hit the joint between the crossbar and the post. The game turned ugly late in the third period when Jarome Iginla confronted Nashville rookie Jordan Tootoo after he knocked over Dean McAmmond. Iginla was cut over the eye in the fracas in which Tootoo started throwing punches before Iginla had a chance to remove his gloves. After the game Iginla said, "He's a young guy. Most guys that fight you have the respect to wait until the other guy's ready but that's the first one that I've been through like that and I'll be ready the next time."

GAME 48
January 24, 2004
Tampa Bay 6 at Calgary 2

Nobody would have seen this mid-January game as a Stanley Cup Final preview. The first period ended 1-1 with the Flames' Dean McAmmond jamming in a rebound after some good work on the power play by Oleg Saprykin and Jordan Leopold. Soon after, Martin St. Louis tied the game when Tampa Bay had the extra man. This goal ended Roman Turek's shutout streak at just less than 125 minutes. The second period proved to be Calgary's undoing as the Lightning outscored the Flames 4-1 and held a 14-7 edge in shots. Speedy forward Martin St. Louis tormented the Flames all night and notched a hat

trick and one assist. It was a satisfying performance for a player who split his first two pro seasons between the Flames and the minors. The Calgary fans grew restless as the game wore on and took to jeering Roman Turek every time he made a save. Turek responded by waiving back to crowd. After the game he quipped, "that was just my reaction. What else am I supposed to do – start crying?" In fairness to Turek, he was suspect on one goal but the others were a result of defensive errors by his teammates. With the loss the Flames fell back into seventh place in the Western Conference behind Nashville. On this night Calgary's key rivals in the standings, the Kings, Coyotes, Stars, and Predators all won which left coach Darryl Sutter grousing after the game.

Flames players pour off the bench to congratulate Shean Donovan whose penalty shot goal proved to be the game winner in the Flames' 2-1 win in Phoenix.

GAME 49

January 27, 2004
Calgary 2 at Phoenix 1

The Flames beat Phoenix for the third straight time courtesy of Shean Donovan's successful penalty shot with 2:08 left in the game. He was awarded the shot after he was taken down by Coyotes' defenseman Ossi Vaananen whose miscue gave Donovan a clear breakaway. The hard-working forward deked Sean Burke beautifully to score his 16th goal in 49 games, quite a feat for someone whose previous season high was 13. Donovan's dramatic winner was his second successful penalty shot of the season. Calgary shouldn't have needed a late winner as the Flames controlled much of the game with a 34-12 edge in shots. Roman Turek gave up a soft goal to Daymond Lankow in the first period but the Flames persevered and outplayed the Coyotes. Jarome Iginla tied the game

at 18:58 of the second period when he capitalized on goalie Sean Burke misplaying the puck behind his own net. The Phoenix netminder cleared the puck onto the stick of Iginla who then raced to the front of the net and tucked it between Burke's pads as he made a desperate attempt to get back into position. Centre Dean McAmmond was unable to finish the game after he was hit by an Iginla shot in the opening period.

GAME 50

January 28, 2004
Calgary 1 at **San Jose 4**

The Flames were soundly beaten in San Jose as they were outplayed and outshot in each period. This continued a frustrating trend for the club of alternating wins and losses. Former Sharks coach Darryl Sutter lost his third straight game in San Jose since taking over the Flames. The Flames

started slowly and did not record their second shot of the game until the 14:57 mark of the first period. The Sharks swarmed the Flames net, which was ably guarded by Roman Turek. He could not be faulted on the screened shot by Mike Rathje that beat him to open the scoring. Calgary had trouble with Patrick Marleau all night as he scored twice, including the game winner. Martin Gelinas was the only Calgary player to find the net behind Evgeni Nabokov. An accidental tip of Gelinas' shot by Sharks rookie Christian Ehrhoff caused the goal, which ended Nabokov's shutout streak at nearly six periods. All night the Sharks forced Calgary into low-percentage shots and controlled most of the rebounds. The Flames did pressure San Jose late in the first but this was enhanced by a series of penalty calls against the home side. Calgary defenceman Rhett Warrener suffered a nasty 35-stitch courtesy of an errant stick.

GAME 51
January 30, 2004
Chicago 5 at Calgary 3

Not only did the Flames drop a home game to one of the worst teams in the league, they also watched Chicago end its 19-game losing streak on the road. This was the worst streak in history of the Hawks franchise and the fourth worst in NHL history. Tuomo Ruutu scored twice as the Flames played very carelessly in their own zone much of the night. The Flames actually held a 3-1 lead before the Hawks scored four unanswered goals. It was Ruutu's second goal off a goalmouth scramble to make the score 3-2 that seemed to ignite Chicago. Jarome Iginla notched two goals and an assist for Calgary and in the process moved past Kent Nilsson into fourth place on the Flames' all-time goal-scoring list with 230. Craig Conroy caused Chicago a few problems early by setting up Iginla and Toni Lydman for goals. Calgary kept pressing, but Steve Passmore made several outstanding saves to keep his club within striking distance. Roman Turek was unable to match his counterpart once the Hawks got rolling and Calgary began falling asleep in its own end. This was a game in which injured defensive centre Stephane Yelle and steady defenseman Rhett Warrener would have been helpful and perhaps settled the team down a bit when the momentum began to shift.

GAME 52
February 1, 2004
Anaheim 4 at **Calgary 6**

The Flames matched their highest scoring out put of the season while vanquishing the Ducks. Chris Clark notched his first career two-goal game while Dean McAmmond scored once and added two assists. Clark was one of several players singled out in the media by Darryl Sutter after the team's poor game against Chicago. The game was more lopsided than the score would indicate as Anaheim used its effective power play to score a couple of goals. Overall the Flames out skated the Ducks and were physically assertive. The line of Martin Gelinas, Shean Donovan, and Dean McAmmond had the better of the play against their counterparts on Anaheim. Much of the Flames' success was built on grit and effort. Assistant coach Rich Preston said after the game, "We'll take the two points. They can't all be Remnbrandts." It was noteworthy that defenseman Mike Commodore played his first game of the season after being called up from the minors. The burly defender would later add depth and grit to the Flames' drive to the Stanley Cup Finals. Roman Turek was on the bench in favour of limping Jamie McLennan as Sutter was concerned that the Czech goalie was becoming a convenient excuse for the team's woes against Tampa Bay and Chicago. As for McLennan, he made all the stops he was supposed to in an efficient if unremarkable performance. Defencemen Robyn Regehr, Toni Lydman, and Jordan Leopold also played well and logged plenty of ice time.

Craig Conroy of Calgary mixes it up with Chicago's Alexei Zhamnov during the Hawks' 5-3 road win at the Saddledome.

Flames' goalie Roman Turek makes the stop on Mark Rycroft of St. Louis during the first period of the Blues' 2-1 road win.

breakaway to make it 4-2 before Calgary allowed goals by Alexander Frolov and Luc Robitaille to tie the game.

GAME 54
February 5, 2004
St. Louis 2 at Calgary 1

For the second time in a week the Flames watched their opponents win a game and end a winless streak. The Blues topped Calgary 2-1 at teh Pengrowth Saddledome to claim their first victory and snap an eight-game losing skid. Calgary's power play was ineffective with only two shots in five man-advantage situations. Overall, the Blues smothered the Flames' offense over the last two periods in this textbook road win. The Flames also did little to challenge Blues goalie Chris Osgood who entered the game having given up eleven goals in his last 68 shots. Instead, the Blues scored first, Keith Tckachuk doing the damage at 8:35 of the second period. Dean McAmmdond scored his 15th of the season to tie game, and that's how the second period ended, 1-1. Scott Mellanby scored the winner with 4:15 left in the third period. He was given a clear shot on goal when McAmmond broke his own stick while trying to battle for the puck. The Flames had a glorious opportunity to tie the game when Dallas Drake was called for boarding at 17:46. They pulled Roman Turek to create a 6-on-4 advantage but were unable to register a shot let alone equalize. In fact, the club mustered a paltry three shots in the final frame. Although he allowed only two goals and was solid in the first period, Turek struggled with rebounds. After this disappointing result, the Flames were left with only three of a possible eight points during a crucial five-game home stand against generally weaker opponents.

GAME 53
February 3, 2004
Los Angeles 4 at Calgary 4

The Flames enjoyed two-goal leads twice but had to settle for a tie with the Kings. Jarome Iginla scored three goals and eight different Calgary players recorded assists, including goalie Jamie McLennan. It was later revealed that McLennan played with a cracked sternum for several games in January to cover for Miikka Kiprusoff and Roman Turek. This was a game the Flames had in hand before the defensive blunders that had been plaguing the club of late resurfaced at critical times. The only good thing

from this point earned was that the Flames gained ground on the slumping St. Louis Blues. McLennan started in net again. His performance was gutsy, but he was obviously playing through pain. At one point, one of his teammates fell on him during a goalmouth scramble but McLennan remained between the pipes. At the other end, Roman Cechmanek was shaky and allowed a dump-in by Jarome Iginla to bounce off his stick into the goal to give Calgary a 2-0 lead. Later, Cechmanek was replaced after he allowed a soft goal to Dean McAmmond to make it 3-2 Flames. Cristobal Huet was quickly faked out of his shorts by Jarome Iginla on a

54th NHL All-Star Game (Xcel Energy Center, Minnesota)

February 8, 2004

 **EASTERN** 6   **WESTERN** 4

Eastern Conference: Joe Thornton (*Boston*), Ilya Kovalchuk (*Atlanta*), Martin St. Louis (*Tampa Bay*), Scott Stevens (*New Jersey*), Scott Niedermayer (*New Jersey*), martin Brodeur (*New Jersey*), Roberto Luongo (*Florida*), Jose Theodore (*Montreal*), Robert Lang (*Washington*), Mats Sundin (*Toronto*), Marian Hossa (*Ottawa*), Jaromir Jagr (*Washington*), Mark Messier (*Rangers*), Daniel Alfredsson (*Ottawa*), Jeremy Roenick (*Philadelphia*), Keith Primeau (*Philadelphia*), Gary Roberts (*Toronto*), Glen Murray (*Boston*), Sheldon Souray (*Montreal*), Adrian Aucoin (*Islanders*), Nick Boynton (*Boston*), Wade Redden (*Ottawa*), Brian Rafalski (*New Jersey*), Pavel Kubina (*Tampa Bay*)

Western Conference: Mike Modano (*Dallas*), Bill Guerin (*Dallas*), Todd Bertuzzi (*Vancouver*), Nicklas Lidstrom (*Detroit*), Rob Blake (*Colorado*), Marty Turco (*Dallas*), Dwayne Roloson (*Minnesota*), Tomas Vokoun (*Nashville*), Shane Doan (*Phoenix*), Pavel Datsyuk (*Detroit*), Markus Naslund (*Vancouver*), Jarome Iginla (*Calgary*), Patrick Marleau (*San Jose*), Rick Nash (*Columbus*), Keith Tkachuk (*St. Louis*), Joe Sakic (*Colorado*), Alex Tanguay (*Colorado*), Kimmo Timonen (*Nashville*), Chris Pronger (*St. Louis*), Mattias Norstrom (*Los Angeles*), Filip Kuba (*Minnesota*)

First Period
1	EASTERN, Aucoin (Messier, Jagr)	5:44
2.	WESTERN, Sakic (Naslund, Bertuzzi)	13:37

penalties: none

Second Period
3.	EASTERN, Alfredsson (unassisted)	1:51
4.	WESTERN, Sakic (Naslund, Bertuzzi)	5:44
5.	WESTERN, Doan (Lidstrom, Tkachuk)	13:02
6.	EASTERN, Messier (Niedermayer, Lang)	13:48
7.	EASTERN, Roberts (Alfredsson, Sundin)	14:41
8.	EASTERN, Alfredsson (Sundin, Roberts)	18:04

penalties: none

Third Period
9.	EASTERN, Kovalchuk (Souray)	4:03
10.	WESTERN, Sakic (Naslund)	7:22

penalties: none

Shots on Goal:
EASTERN	10	12	7	**29**
WESTERN	11	12	9	**32**

Goalies:
EASTERN	Brodeur (1st period, one goal)
EASTERN	Theodore (2nd period, two goals)
EASTERN	Luongo (3rd period, one goal)
WESTERN	Turco (1st period, one goal)
WESTERN	Vokoun (2nd period, four goals)
WESTERN	Roloson (3rd period, one goal)

Referees	Blaine Angus, Stephen Walkom
Linesmen	Scott Driscoll, Thor Nelson
Attendance	19,434
MVP:	Joe Sakic (*Colorado*)

Flames captain Jarome Iginla participated in the shooting accuracy contest in the Super Skills competition at All-Star weekend and then played for the Western Conference the next afternoon. Teammate Matt Lombardi skated in the YoungStars Game as well this weekend.

GAME 55

February 10, 2004
Atlanta 2 at **Calgary 5**

The Flames defeated an Atlanta Thrashers team that included Dany Heatley in the lineup. It was Heatley's first game in his hometown since the tragic accident on the eve of the 2003-04 season. Dean McAmmond and Jarome Iginla scored two goals each to lead Calgary. More significantly, future playoff hero Miikka Kiprusoff returned from the injured list and stopped 23 of 25 shots to backstop his club's win. In fact, the Calgary goalie kept his team in the game during a poor first period when defensive miscues provided the Thrashers with several golden opportunities, two of which were buried by Ilya Kovalchuk. One of the few bright moments in that frame was Shean Donovan's hustle, which provided Dean McAmmond with an open net on which to score. The Flames were much sharper in the second period and tied the game on a nifty three-way passing play between Chris Clark, Steve Reinprecht, and goal scorer Matthew Lombardi. An oddity in the game occurred when Heatley set up Kovalchuk's second goal, but his name was accidentally omitted in the public address announcement of the scoring play. The Saddledome crowd was actually more concerned and upset with Kovalchuk after he stayed down on the ice on two occasions hoping to draw a penalty. The Flames salted the win in the third period when Jarome Iginla lifted a backhand over Pasi Nurminen after he and linemates Craig Conroy and Oleg Saprykin forechecked Atlanta relentlessly. Kiprusoff's return did not come a moment too soon. At the time of his injury, the Flames were nine games over .500 but struggled with a 7-10-2 mark with Roman Turek and the brave but injury-plagued play of Jamie McLennan in goal.

GAME 56

February 11, 2004
Calgary 3 at Vancouver 2

Jarome Iginla's goal at 0:28 of the third period gave the Flames a key win in Vancouver. The result gave the Flames five wins and a tie in their last six games against the Canucks in Vancouver. Iginla's goal was his sixth in the past four games. The much-maligned Roman Turek made 32 saves including 13 in the third period. His biggest save came in the first when he robbed Todd Bertuzzi with the Canucks already ahead 2-0. Rather than face a three-goal deficit, Calgary was back in game at 2-1 as Craig Conroy scored ten seconds after Turek's heroics. Calgary was down 2-0 as a result of running into penalty trouble against one of the top power play units in the NHL. Dean McAmmond received four minutes (two for slashing and two for arguing the call) then Rhett Warrener was whistled for slashing Todd Bertuzzi as they battled in front of the net. Sami Salo scored with the two man advantage, and then Jarkko Ruutu's shot bounced up and over Turek as the second penalty expired. The Flames' power play tied the game courtesy of Chuck Kobasew. On the third period winner, Iginla corralled the puck in the corner and moved in front of the net before snapping a shot off the post and in behind Dan Cloutier. Turek wasn't through as he made a diving glove save on Brendan Morrison from close range on a Vancouver power play with 2:22 left in the game to preserve the win.

GAME 57

February 13, 2004
Anaheim 1 at **Calgary 2**

The Flames topped the Ducks for the second time in two weeks. Jarome Iginla's second period power play goal stood up as the winner. Miikka Kiprusoff turned in a solid perform-

Shean Donovan tries to score on a wraparound as Vancouver goalie Dan Cloutier gets his stick down to keep the puck out. The teams tied 4-4.

Flames defenceman Denis Gauthier ties up his man, Anaheim's Petr Sykora, during Calgary's 2-1 win at the Saddledome.

ance by stopping 25 of 26 shots. He made ten saves in the final period and none was bigger than when he snared Vitaly Vishnevki's rising backhander with the Ducks pressing. The Flames power play did its job by scoring both goals and finishing 2-for-6 on the night. On the opening goal, Jordan Leopold's shot eluded Jean-Sebastien Giguere after Calgary clogged the front of the net with traffic. Iginla's marker came on a nice feed from Craig Conroy during a two-man advantage. Anaheim was credited with a power play goal of its own after a video review showed that Steve Rucchin's quick shot crossed the line before coming out. There was little flow during the first half of the game as the officials called nine minors. The Ducks threatened the Calgary goal early in the third period as the Flames seemed a bit jittery. Eventually they settled down and benefited from Kiprusoff's steady play to climb nine games above .500 for the first time since their starting goalie went down with an injury several weeks earlier.

GAME 58
February 15, 2004
Calgary 2 at Minnesota 1

The Flames won their fourth straight game since the All-Star break and their 30th of the season to surpass their win total for all of 2002-03. In so doing they climbed to ten games over .500 for the first time in eleven seasons. Miikka Kiprusoff continued to excel, though this was a dull game in which each team recorded only 16 shots on net. The game was also a matchup between Kiprusoff and Dwayne Roloson, the owners of the two best save percentages in the NHL. Jarome Iginla opened the scoring after Craig Conroy feathered a beautiful pass from behind the net and past three Minnesota checkers. This goal was a back breaker in a tight game as it came in the last minute of the period. The power play notched both goals, the game winner coming from Robyn Regehr at 6:25 of the third period on a set up from Dean McAmmond. Regehr sent a wrist shot toward the goal, which went between Martin Gelinas' legs and into the Minnesota net. It was a satisfying win for the Flames as they gave last year's Western Conference finalists a taste of their own medicine. Calgary played air-tight defense while striking when a rare opportunity emerged. The win solidified the Flames' hold on fifth place in the conference as they moved four points ahead of the Dallas Stars and Los Angeles Kings.

GAME 59

February 19, 2004
Calgary 1 at **Montreal 4**

The Flames generated only 20 shots and few scoring chances in dropping a 4-1 road decision to Montreal. A win would have given the club its first five-game winning streak since 1996-97. Yet it was the Canadiens that came out flying as they tried to end a season-high four-game losing streak. The high point for Calgary was the first period when the Flames played the Habs even 1-1 and Jarome Iginla reached the 30-goal mark for the fourth consecutive season. His goal came with the teams playing 4-on-4 as he blew past Patrice Brisebois and ripped a slapshot over the right shoulder of Montreal backup goalie Mathieu Garon. The Flames enjoyed a couple of spurts in the third period but the steady Garon held his ground.

Toni Lydman shows his slapshot form from the top of the circle.

Flames defenceman Andrew Ference (centre) clears the puck before a New Jersey forward can get a shot on goal.

He robbed Denis Gauthier with a brilliant glove save midway through the third and shut the door twice on Jarome Iginla later in the same sequence. Curiously, many members of the Montreal crowd chose to focus on booing Saku Koivu after two over-publicized altercations during practise with leading scorer Mike Ribeiro. The top Calgary skater was Gauthier who was one of the few Flames to play a robust defensive game and make offensive forays at the appropriate time.

GAME 60

February 21, 2004
Calgary 1 at **Ottawa 2**

Calgary's visit to the Corel Centre was the first game in the annual *Hockey Day In Canada* triple-header involving all six Canadian clubs. The Flames lost after Martin Havlat beat Roman Turek at 2:26 of the third period. Many Calgary players claimed that the play was offside but the goal stood. Jordan Leopold scored for the Flames but the stingy Senators halted Jarome Iginla's five game goal-scoring streak. Calgary's top two forward lines were closely checked all night and rarely threat-

ened Patrick Lalime through the first two periods. The Flames opened the scoring when Jordan Leopold's stoppable wrist shot on the power play eluded Patrick Lalime. Calgary could not make this lead hold up as the club lacked discipline in the first period. They were whistled for three straight penalties and finally paid the price on the third man advantage situation when Bryan Smolinski tipped Daniel Alfredsson's point shot past Turek. On the plus side, the Flames played with more grit along the boards and won quite a few of the little battles that often influence the outcome of a game. After Havlat's goal, Calgary went on the attack and put some pressure on the Senators' defense. With Turek on bench, Jordan Leopold was left uncovered in the slot but was stopped cold by Lalime to preserve the Ottawa win.

GAME 61

February 22, 2004
Calgary 1 at **New Jersey 3**

For the second straight game a top notch defensive club stifled the Flames. The Flames recorded only 19 shots with Chuck Kobasew proving to be the only player to beat

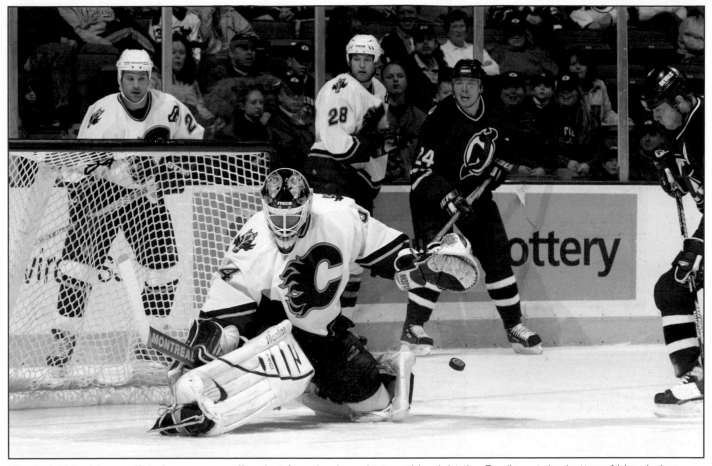

Goalie Miikka Kiprusoff makes a save off a shot from in close, but on this night the Devils got the better of him during their 3-1 win over the visiting Flames.

Devils' ace goalie Martin Brodeur. Kobasew's goal came on a rebound off Toni Lydman's shot after he charged to the net on a Calgary power play. It was one of the few dangerous moments around the Devils' net in this game as New Jersey played a solid defensive game and often kept Calgary bottled up in its own end. Patrick Elias scored twice for the home team and combined with Brian Gionta and Scott Gomez to give the Calgary defense trouble all night. The Flames power play counted one goal but was unable to cash in when it had a chance to alter the course of the game. The unit failed to score on a five-minute power play after New Jersey's Colin White was whistled for high sticking Denis Gauthier. Pouring salt on the wound was the fact that the short-handed Devils outshot Calgary 5-0 during this stretch. Shortly after the five-minute major

expired, Andrew Ference was unable to cover Patrick Elias who easily finished off a play with Scott Gomez and Jamie Langenbrunner. After opening the season 9-1 against Eastern Conference opponents, the Flames dropped to 1-5-1 in their last seven inter-conference encounters.

GAME 62
February 24, 2004
Calgary 2 at Colorado 0

The Flames ended their three-game losing streak by shutting down the skilled Avalanche in Denver. The win came on the second anniversary of Canada's gold medal triumph over the United States at the 2002 Salt Lake City Olympics. Miikka Kiprusoff stopped all 26 shots that were sent his way and Martin Gelinas notched game winner with 2:19 left in the third period. Chris Clark added empty net

insurance and the team was helped by Stephane Yelle who returned to action after recovering from a knee injury. The Avalanche threatened in the first period on two power plays but could not score. Kiprusoff made a cat-like grab off a Riku Hahl shot then received help from the goalpost to keep the game scoreless after one period. In the second, he stoned Milan Hejduk on a 3-on-2 rush. Calgary had the better chances in the third and opened the scoring when Craig Conroy centred a pass that Martin Gelinas tried to knock down so he could take a shot. Instead, the puck bounced off his torso and landed behind a startled David Aebischer. Former Avalanche checker Stephane Yelle made a key shot block that enabled Chris Clark to head up ice and score into the empty net. In the tight Western Conference standings, this victory vaulted the Flames from eighth to fifth.

GAME 63

February 26, 2004
Detroit 2 at Calgary 1

The Flames returned from their mediocre five game road trip (2-3-0) and dropped a tight contest to the efficient Red Wings. Detroit didn't play superbly but the Wings scored when they needed to and relied on 33 saves from Manny Legace. The fact that the Flames started slowly but began to play harder as the game wore on did not impress assistant coach Jim Playfair. He angrily noted, "We can't dial it in every once in a while. We have to compete and practice with a sense of urgency every day." The Flames were being shut out until Chuck Kobasew finally scored for the home side with 7:51 left in the game. Calgary went 0-for-5 on the power play as the Wings gladly gave up the perimeter but guarded the ice near the net very carefully. The Stanley Cup champions from 2002 showed the Flames how to play a sensible road game and punish an opponent via a quick counter-attack. This was clear on Detroit's first goal when Denis Gauthier sent a careless pass up the middle of the ice, which was picked off by Pavel Datsyuk. He moved up ice with Henrik Zetterberg who fed a perfect pass to Ray Whitney. On the second goal, Matthew Lombardi lost the puck at his own blueline to Datsyuk who fed it over to Brett Hull and Steve Thomas for a two-on-nothing break that saw the latter finish off the scoring play. Kobasew brought the home side to within a goal as his screen shot beat Manny Legace.

GAME 64

February 29, 2004
Phoenix 2 at **Calgary 4**

The Flames scored three goals in the first 15:44 then hung on to beat Phoenix 4-2. This was only the second Leap Year Day game since the

Jarome Iginla (centre) is mobbed by teammates Toni Lydman (left) and Steve Reinprecht (right) after a goal.

club moved to Calgary. For the record, they topped the Pittsburgh Penguins 7-3 eight years ago. There were a couple of different Calgary teams playing this evening. After showing initiative in the first period, the Flames sat back and allowed Phoenix to take the play. In the first frame, Jarome Iginla ended a four-game goal drought and the club received an offensive boost from the blueline with goals from Robyn Regehr and Jordan Leopold. Shane Doan closed the gap to 3-2 but the Flames settled down and outshot the Coyotes 12-3 in the third period. Chuck Kobasew added an insurance goal with less than five minutes remaining with his fourth goal in the last nine games. Toni Lydman enjoyed a solid game and led all Flames with 21:46 of ice time. All

but five players recorded at least one shot on net in this win which left the Flames on pace for the 90-point output most experts felt was required to make the playoffs in the Western Conference.

GAME 65

March 2, 2004
Calgary 4 at St. Louis 2

Two goals and an assist from Jarome Iginla powered the Flames past a St. Louis club that was still dealing with the firing of coach Joel Quenneville. Miikka Kiprusoff had to be sharp as the Blues registered 30 shots. The Flames started slowly with only one shot in the first fifteen minutes. They later took over a tight game with four third-period goals. Trailing 1-0 early in the third, super-pest Ville Nieminen knocked over goalie Chris Osgood who was unable to get back to his net before Steve Reinprecht registered his first goal since November 22. Osgood and the Blues were furious that a penalty was not called and seemed to lose their focus after that. Iginla made it 2-1 moments later but the Blues equalized via a Pavol Demitra power-play goal. Undaunted, the Flames persisted and won on goals by Iginla, who outhustled the St. Louis defense to score on his own rebound, and Reinprecht, who clinched the game with an empty netter. The Flames came out of this game with an 18-3-2-1 record in games where Iginla scores. More importantly, they seemed to show a killer instinct and seized control of the game after Nieminen's controversial run-in with Osgood. The game also marked the 22nd time in 25 starts that Miikka Kiprusoff surrendered two or fewer goals.

GAME 66
March 3, 2004
Calgary 1 at **Detroit 2**

The Flames dropped another squeaker to the Wings despite outshooting the home team 29-22. Manny Legace confounded the Calgary shooters again and only Jarome Iginla found the back of the net, at 15:01 of the third period. Just as in the previous 2-1 loss to Detroit on February 26, the Flames failed to score on all five of their power-play opportunities. The Flames thought they caught a break when the Wings' gritty Kris Draper hurt his rotator cuff in practice and was unable to dress. As it often turns out with elite teams, however, Draper's replacement, Mark Mowers, counted the decisive goal. Though somewhat fatigued from the previous night's win in St. Louis, the Flames carried the play to Detroit in the first period. They out shot the Wings 12-5 but were unable to beat Legace. Just past the midpoint of the game, Turek gave up a big rebound on an unscreened Mathieu Schneider shot, which found its way to Henrik Zetterberg for an easy goal. Mowers roofed a backhander over Turek in the third period to put the game seemingly out of reach. Jarome Iginla scored on a fine individual effort to give the Flames some hope but the club shot itself in the foot by icing the puck twice in the last minute to kill any hope of an equalizer.

Mark Mowers scores the game-winning goal in the third period to give the Wings a narrow 2-1 win over the visiting Flames.

Shean Donovon is stopped by Marty Turco on a penalty shot during the second period of the Stars' 5-1 win over the visiting Flames.

GAME 67

March 5, 2004
Calgary 1 at **Dallas 5**

Calgary was unable to beat the Dallas Stars, one of the hottest home teams in the league. Even Miikka Kiprusoff was unable to stem the tide as the Flames gave up 34 shots, many of which were quality chances. The Flames' power-play unit was ineffective once again with no goals from seven opportunities while Dallas scored twice. The poor special teams performance left Calgary with only one goal with the extra man in the last 28 opportunities. The Flames seem to tire with the rash of penalties and the third game in four nights on the road. "It's tough on the team," said Shean Donovan afterward. "There's no flow. We have to get back to playing five-on-five." The first Dallas goal was scored on a quick one-timer by Mike Modano with the Flames two men short. They found themselves in this situation after being hit with their NHL-leading 21st bench minor for having too many men on the ice. After Pierre Turgeon made it 2-0, Rhett Warrener startled Marty Turco with a long shot from outside the blueline. Shean Donovan was given a glorious chance to tie the game late in the second period when he was awarded a penalty shot for the third time this season. Unfortunately, he failed to get a shot away when the puck caught a rut in the ice as he prepared to shoot. The Flames ran out of steam in the third period and gave up three goals, which left them with at least five goals against for only the fourth time in this season.

GAME 68

March 7, 2004
Calgary 7 at Colorado 1

The day after acquiring hard-nosed forward Chris Simon from the New York Rangers, the Flames embarrassed the Avalanche 7-1 in Denver. It was a huge victory for the Flames who showed signs of growing as a team by putting the disappointing score in Dallas behind them. In the process they handed Colorado its worst regular season loss in nearly five years. Calgary started quickly but was not rewarded with a goal initially. In fact, the Flames trailed 1-0 after Milan Hejduk scored on a power play with Krzysztof Oliwa in the penalty box. Jordan Leopold tied the game on a nice feed from Steve Reinprecht to give the Flames something to show for their solid opening period. Chris Clark put the Flames ahead to stay by charging the net from the corner untouched and jamming the puck past Philippe Sauve. This goal was indicative of the passive resistance put forth by Colorado in their own zone much of the night. Jarome Iginla scored his 35th goal, a short-handed tally, and then Craig Conroy broke the Avalanche's back when his shot was accidentally tipped by the normally reliable Adam Foote into his net to make the score 4-1. Oliwa made it 5-1 and Oleg Saprykin scored twice late in the game to finish off the route.

GAME 69

March 9, 2004

Edmonton 1 at **Calgary 1**

This edition of the Battle of Alberta was a tense affair as the Flames tried to solidify their playoff spot while the Oilers remained five points out of a post-season spot. The heated rivalry was quickly evident when Krzysztof Oliwa tripped Jason Smith on an icing call causing the Edmonton blueliner to crash dangerously into the boards. There were no goals through the first 40 minutes, although the Oilers had the better chances early. Ville Nieminen opened the scoring in the third when he out-muscled Mike York and pounced on a rebound to beat Markkanen. Nieminen's goal was his first as a Flame and his first in 33 games dating back to December 21 when he was still with the Chicago Blackhawks. Shawn Horcoff equalized at 9:53 of the final frame to give the visitors a valuable point. The tying goal was upsetting for the Flames as they failed to cover up a rebound after Miikka Kiprusoff made a tough save on a deflected shot by Cory Cross. In the extra period, Calgary was forced to kill off a 4-on-3 short-handed situation. Stephane Yelle and Kiprusoff were brilliant in this stretch to deny the Oilers a win. Jussi Markkanen was brilliant in net and seemed to justify the Oilers' trading Tommy Salo to give him more playing time. The tie left the Flames in sole possession of sixth place in the Western Conference standings.

GAME 70

March 11, 2004

Ottawa 2 at **Calgary 4**

This win was a solid confidence builder for the Flames as they were full value for a 4-2 decision over a bona fide Stanley Cup contender. Calgary opened the scoring with a makeshift power-play unit of goal scorer Markus Nilson with Chuck Kobasew and Ville Nieminen. Nieminen missed on his initial shot but recovered the puck and sent it back to Toni Lydman on the point whose shot was tipped in by Nilson. In the second period, Marian Hossa tied the game on a Senators power play before the Flames wasted three consecutive opportunities with the extra man. It took fourth liners Krzysztof Oliwa and Matthew Lombardi to give Ottawa a 2-1 lead with the big enforcer counting his second goal in three games. The Flames outshot Ottawa 14-8 in the third period but the Sens tied the game when Denis Gauthier pinched at the Ottawa blueline at an ill-advised time and Martin Havlat was able to bury his breakaway gift. Ville Nieminen broke the 2-2 tie at the 9:16 mark after beating his check and roofing one into the net. Marcus Nilson's second goal of the game into an empty net ensured a Calgary win and continued his run of good play since joining the Flames.

Even on his belly, Flames' goalie Miikka Kiprusoff manages to make a great pad save on Ryan Smyth of the Oilers during their 1-1 tie.

GAME 71

March 13, 2004
Calgary 4 at Nashville 4

After the Todd Bertuzzi assault on Steve Moore and with Jordan Tootoo a healthy scratch, there was less likelihood of this game getting out of hand despite the bad blood that emerged from the previous meeting between these two teams. This was a fast-skating affair with Calgary newcomers Markus Nilson, Chris Simon, and Ville Nieminen all scoring. The latter continued his fine play for Darryl Sutter after spending most of the year in Brian Sutter's doghouse while still in Chicago. Nilson opened the scoring 26 seconds into the game after he pounced on a Shean Donovan rebound to beat Tomas Vokoun. Nashville scored the next three goals before Nieminen jammed home a goal at 18:38 of the second while on his knees after Donovan did much of the spade - work to control the puck. Only 34 seconds later, Kiprusoff fed the puck to Craig Conroy who hit Simon with a perfect pass. The burly forward made no mistake and put a backhand behind Vokoun. The teams entered the final period tied 3-3 before exchanging goals in the first minute, including Iginla's 36th of the season. The Predators' hot new acquisition, Steve Sullivan, narrowly missed winning the game in overtime but his shot from the slot sailed over the crossbar.

GAME 72

March 14, 2004
Calgary 3 at St. Louis 0

Roman Turek continued up-and-down season by stopping all 25 shots to lead Calgary to victory over the Blues. For the second straight game Marcus Nilson scored early to give the Flames a 1-0 advantage. St. Louis came out with more jump in the second period, but the Flames weathered the storm and went ahead 2-0 when Craig Conroy tried to deflect Jordan Leopold's shot from the point but missed and was the benefactor of a lucky bounce off his foot. In the third period, the Flames played solid defense in limiting St. Louis to seven shots. Turek remained steady and Chris Simon scored into an empty net with some help from Jarome Iginla. This was the Blues' first defeat since losing to the Flames on March 2. The win brought the Flames' point total to 82 and ensured them of at least a .500 season for the first time since 1994-95. In addition, the Flames were able to secure three of a possible four points on the road against two clubs battling them for a playoff spot. They played smart, disciplined hockey and limited their dangerous opponent to only three power-play opportunities all night. St. Louis goalie Chris Osgood took the loss and remained one win shy of 300 in his career.

Marcus Nilson of Calgary beats Tomas Vokoun of Nashville with a shot during the first period of a 4-4 tie between the Flames and Predators.

Stophane Yelle beats Manny Legace with a shot as Kirk Maltby looks on during first period action of Calgary's 4-1 win over the Red Wings.

GAME 73

March 16, 2004
Calgary 4 at Detroit 1

Miikka Kiprusoff stopped 25 of 26 shots to lead the Flames to a big win over Detroit. During the course of the season, the Flames had managed to secure at least one win against all of the NHL's top clubs – except for Detroit. They lost all three previous games by falling behind and being stifled by solid goaltending and the Wings' disciplined play. A sign that things might be different this game came in the first period when Calgary was outshot 10-1 but scored the only goal when a puck fired by Jordan Leopold hit Stephane Yelle's skate and bounced behind Manny Legace. A replacement for the injured Toni Lydman, Steve Montador scored the decisive goal after sitting out 16 straight games. Afterward, the excited Montador described Calgary's strategy; "We definitely wanted to frustrate them with a good forecheck and good speed." Goals by Matthew Lombardi

and Detroit's Kirk Maltby left the score at 3-1 midway in the third period. Late in the game, Craig Conroy finished off a pretty 2-on-1 with Ville Nieminen to close the book on this solid effort. The Flames were full value for this win as their speed and urgency made the Wings look old and slow. The seeds were planted for this club to have renewed confidence against Detroit when the clubs met in the second round of the playoffs.

GAME 74

March 18, 2004
Columbus 0 at **Calgary 2**

Hot goalie Miikka Kiprusoff notched his third shutout of the year and lowered his NHL-best goals-against average to 1.63. In defeating Columbus, the Flames remained unbeaten in a season-high seven games at a critical juncture of the schedule. This was an important two points for the Flames as they faced a beatable opponent at home after a

successful road swing. Matthew Lombardi's second-period goal was all Calgary needed. Lombardi was in the right spot after Denis Gauthier's shot hit Columbus defenseman Duvie Westcott and landed in front of him. Despite the Flames' territorial edge in play, Jackets goalie Marc Denis was the star of the show making 23 saves after two periods. Calgary was not discouraged by the hot goalie and continued to press for an insurance goal. Yet, the Flames could not solve Denis and had to kill a penalty in the last minute when Ville Nieminen was called for hooking. Their penalty killing rose to the occasion and Jarome Iginla fired home a short-handed, empty-net goal to clinch matters. That goal was his 37th of the season and brought him within one of league leader Ilya Kovalchuk of the Atlanta Thrashers. The win vaulted the Flames seven points clear of a playoff spot and moved them within two points of Vancouver and a chance at securing home ice advantage in the post-season.

Nashville goalie Tomas Vokoun makes the save as his teammates prevent Chris Clark of Calgary from getting near the puck.

GAME 75
March 20, 2004
Nashville 3 at Calgary 1

The bad blood between these two clubs boiled over a week later than some expected as the Flames vented their frustration at losing an important home game. Overall, Nashville won more of the battles in the trenches as the Predators fought desperately to end a seven-game winless streak. The game started well for the Flames when Jarome Iginla tipped Steve Montador's point shot past Tomas Vokoun on a power play at 3:23 of the first period. With only 0.5 seconds left in the first, Scott Hartnell deflated the Flames by tying the game after flattening Denis Gauthier

to claim the puck. Martin Erat gave Nashville a well deserved lead late in the second period as he found an opening when Miikka Kiprusoff failed to cover the post. In the final period, the Flames were completely shut down by Nashville and could muster only two shots. The visitors clinched the win with Sergei Zholtok's empty-net goal. On the ensuing face off, coach Darryl Sutter sent out a makeshift forward line of enforcer Krzysztof Oliwa with rugged blueliners Robyn Regehr and Mike Commodore. The resulting melee involved everyone on the ice including goalies Kiprusoff and Vokoun.

GAME 76
March 22, 2004
Dallas 4 at Calgary 0

This was not the kind of game the home side was looking to play. Coach Darryl Sutter had to watch the game from the press box after being handed a two-game suspension for his lineup decision at the end of the previous game versus Nashville. The club came out flat in the first period and was outscored 3-0 and outshot 15-4. Shayne Corson's opening goal symbolized the night as he out-worked Calgary's defense to score on a wraparound. On the second goal, Brendan Morrow was left alone in front of the net for an easy score after Denis Gauthier got tangled up behind the net. Midway through the first period, any chance for the Flames to gain some life was quelled when Marcus Nilson was judged to have kicked the puck into the goal off a Shean Donovan pass. A short time later, the Flames were down by three as Rhett Warrener lost the puck to Jason Arnott deep in his own zone. Calgary outshot Dallas 25-9 the rest of the way, but Marty Turco had a decent view of most of the shots headed his way. The final insult came when the Flames pulled Miikka Kiprusoff only to have an errant pass by Chris Clark go into their own net. The goal was credited to Corson.

GAME 77

March 24, 2004
Calgary 4 at Phoenix 0

Two nights after a dismal 4-0 loss at home, the Flames easily turned aside Phoenix by the same score. The enigmatic Roman Turek earned his second straight shutout and seemed much more relaxed away from the Saddledome. Marcus Nilson opened the scoring yet again when he one-timed a quick feed from Ville Nieminen at 11:11 of the first period. Jarome Iginla and Craig Conroy both enjoyed two point nights. Iginla's goal was his 39th and tied him for the NHL lead. Conroy's first goal came on a nifty 2-on-1 break with Iginla. It was also Conroy's first shift after leaving the game with a cut near his eye courtesy of the Coyotes' Krys Kolanos. This game also showcased Iginla's speed and tenacity. Craig Conroy won a face off in the Calgary zone, which Iginla promptly took up ice and managed to squeeze between the boards and defenseman Radoslav Suchy before beating netminder Brent Johnson. Turek may have felt some satisfaction in beating Johnson, the youngster who took his job in St. Louis not so long ago. The Flames

registered 31 shots, were 1-for-3 on the power play and stymied Phoenix on three Coyote man advantages. Calgary won its 21st road game of the year to come within one of the franchise record attained four times during the glory years of the late 1980s and early '90s.

GAME 78

March 25, 2004
Calgary 2 at **San Jose 3**

At this late stage of the season, a plausible first round playoff match up looked to be Calgary versus San Jose. The two teams were very cagey, as each seemed to scouting each other in this game as the post-season loomed. The media coverage surrounding the build up to this game also felt like a playoff encounter. Calgary fell behind 2-0 as a result of two defensive miscues. First, Robyn Regehr left the slot

to help along the boards, which gave Nils Ekman plenty of time to score. On the second goal, Andrew Ference allowed Mike Ricci to get in front of the net where he tipped a shot past a helpless Miikka Kiprusoff. The Flames squandered several power-play chances and seemed doomed to lose until Martin Gelinas redirected Chris Clark's wrist shot behind Evgeni Nabokov midway through the third period. A few minutes later, the Flames finally struck with the extra man when Oleg Saprykin grabbed Jordan Leopold's wide shot and surprised Nabokov. After scoring twice in the last 6:16 of the game to tie the score, the Flames were victimized when Vincent Damphousse scored the winner at 19:36. Miikka Kiprusoff was enjoying a solid game against his former team until Damphousse grabbed a loose puck and fired it recklessly at the net only to have it carom in off the stunned goalic's leg.

Goalie Miikka Kiprusoff stymies Mike Ricci of the Sharks during first-period action in San Jose. The Sharks managed a 3-2 win.

GAME 79

March 27, 2004
Los Angeles 2 at **Calgary 3**
(Donovan 1:06 OT)

Shean Donovan provided the heroics by scoring at 1:06 of overtime to help the Flames inch closer to a playoff spot. The afternoon game was televised in the United States and underscored the Flames' rise to prominence. This was a frustrating game for the Flames and the Saddledome crowd as the visitors were aggressive and clutched-and-grabbed to slow down Calgary's speedy forwards. Adding further insult was the fact that the Kings ended up with one more power-play chance when all was said and done. Los Angeles super-pest Sean Avery opened the scoring and gave his club a 1-0 lead after the first period. Calgary equalized in the second when Chris Simon, soon after having a goal waved off for kicking the puck in, was credited with a score after Jordan Leopold's shot hit him in the shin and bounced past Cristobal Huet. An Andrew Ference giveaway led to the Kings' go-ahead goal by enforcer Jeff Cowan. Craig Conroy got the Flames back on even terms when he beat Huet with a wrist shot through his legs. Both teams were tentative in the third period and seemed content to earn a point. Conroy was in on the overtime winner when he chipped the puck ahead to Shean Donovan who sent the Saddledome crowd into a frenzy with his OT score.

GAME 80

March 31, 2004
Phoenix 0 at **Calgary 1**

With two games to spare the Flames clinched their first playoff appearance in seven years. Two recurring themes were in full view as Jarome Iginla scored his 40th goal and Miikka Kiprusoff stopped 27 shots to

Phoenix goalie Brent Johnson stops Jarome Iginla in close during Calgary's 1-0 home win.

register a shutout. Iginla scored the game's only goal by tipping in Robyn Regehr's centring pass on a first period power-play. Kiprusoff set the tone earlier by stopping Phoenix sniper Shane Doan at point-blank range. Calgary pressed for more goals but Brent Johnson kept things close with a series of tough saves. Kiprusoff took over the show in the third period. The Coyotes put up a fight with 14 shots in the final frame, including a handful of scoring chances after Martin Gelinas was penalized for slashing at 14:28. It was good news all 'round as the crowd of 18,419 represented Calgary's tenth straight sellout. Iginla addressed the team's mood by saying, "This is our first goal – now we prepare for the playoffs." During the course of the game the Flames did many little things well that would later help in the

post-season. Notably, they won 57% of their faceoffs, Craig Conroy leading the way with a stunning 68% success rate.

GAME 81

April 2, 2004
Calgary 3 at Los Angeles 2

There was no letdown for the Flames after clinching a playoff spot. They simply caught a plane to Los Angeles and played an effective road game, winning 3-2 and limiting the Kings to 15 shots. In the process, they equalled the franchise record of 22 road wins in a season. Jeff Cowan opened the scoring for the Kings in the first period, just as a 5-on-3 power play was ending. Martin Gelinas tied the game at 17:21 when

Calgary forwards Krzysztof Oliwa (on one knee) and Chuck Kobasew try in vain to score the tying goal in Anaheim's 2-1 win as goalie Jean-Sebastien Giguere holds the fort in the final minute of play.

he outskated the Kings defender to get open for Chris Clark's quick pass. Only a minute later, Eric Belanger restored the L.A. lead courtesy of a centring pass from Sean Avery. The Flames took over much of the play after that point. Matthew Lombardi scored the tying goal on a power play when Jordan Leopold faked a shot and then feathered a pass to a wide open Lombardi. He notched the winner with 6:06 to go in the third when Gelinas' speed confounded the Kings' defense and left Lombardi open for a perfect pass. Jarome Iginla fired seven shots at Cristobal Huet but was unable to score and claim the outright NHL goal-scoring lead. This was Miikka Kiprusoff's last appearance in the regular season. He finished with a 1.69 goals - against average in 38 games, a modern-day, NHL record, surpassing Marty Turco's 1.72 mark in 2002-03.

The win gave the Flames 94 points and clinched sixth place in the Western Conference.

GAME 82
April 4, 2004
Calgary 1 at **Anaheim 2**

Though the Flames ended the highly successful 2003-04 regular season on a losing note, Jarome Iginla notched his 41st goal to tie Rick Nash and Ilya Kovalchuk for the league lead in goals and a share of the Rocket Richard Trophy. This was only the second three-way tie for the NHL goal scoring lead in history (Charlie Simmer, Danny Gare, and Blaine Stoughton tied in 1979-80). Iginla's 41st was not cheap. He sped down the ice with the Flames short-handed and fired a shot between Jean-Sebastien Giguere's pads to give Calgary a 1-0 lead. The Ducks

prevailed after two, third-period goals less than two minutes apart. Vaclav Prospal's was a quick shot to the roof of the net when Turek fell away from the post slightly. The winner, by veteran Sergei Fedorov, was a seeing-eye backhand that went through several players, including the Calgary netminder. Coach Darryl Sutter elected to give Miikka Kiprusoff a rest before the playoffs and Roman Turek turned in a solid effort in a losing cause. Before Prospal and Fedorov scored in the third period, Turek had not allowed a goal in the previous 160:07. At the other end of the ice, Giguere, the 2003 Conn Smythe Trophy winner, was in fine form as he stoned the Flames as they buzzed the net in hope of gaining a tie. With a first-round matchup with the Vancouver Canucks on the horizon, the Flames showed good jump in a meaningless game.

Final NHL Standings, Regular Season, 2003-04

EASTERN CONFERENCE
ATLANTIC DIVISION

	GP	W	L	T	OTL	PTS	GF	GA
PHILADELPHIA	82	40	21	15	6	101	229	186
NEW JERSEY	82	43	25	12	2	100	213	164
NY ISLANDERS	82	38	29	11	4	91	237	210
NY RANGERS	82	27	40	7	8	69	206	250
PITTSBURGH	82	23	47	8	4	58	190	303

NORTHEAST DIVISION

	GP	W	L	T	OTL	PTS	GF	GA
BOSTON	82	41	19	15	7	104	209	188
TORONTO	82	45	24	10	3	103	242	204
OTTAWA	82	43	23	10	6	102	262	189
MONTREAL	82	41	30	7	4	93	208	192
BUFFALO	82	37	34	7	4	85	220	221

SOUTHEAST DIVISION

	GP	W	L	T	OTL	PTS	GF	GA
TAMPA BAY	82	46	22	8	6	106	245	192
ATLANTA	82	33	37	8	4	78	214	243
CAROLINA	82	28	34	14	6	76	172	209
FLORIDA	82	28	35	15	4	75	188	221
WASHINGTON	82	23	46	10	3	59	186	253

WESTERN CONFERENCE
CENTRAL DIVISION

	GP	W	L	T	OTL	PTS	GF	GA
DETROIT	82	48	21	11	2	109	255	189
ST. LOUIS	82	39	30	11	2	91	191	198
NASHVILLE	82	38	29	11	4	91	216	217
COLUMBUS	82	25	45	8	4	62	177	238
CHICAGO	82	20	43	11	8	59	188	259

NORTHWEST DIVISION

	GP	W	L	T	OTL	PTS	GF	GA
VANCOUVER	82	43	24	10	5	101	235	194
COLORADO	82	40	22	13	7	100	236	198
CALGARY	**82**	**42**	**30**	**7**	**3**	**94**	**200**	**176**
EDMONTON	82	36	29	12	5	89	221	208
MINNESOTA	82	30	29	20	3	83	188	183

PACIFIC DIVISION

	GP	W	L	T	OTL	PTS	GF	GA
SAN JOSE	82	43	21	12	6	104	219	183
DALLAS	82	41	26	13	2	97	194	175
LOS ANGELES	82	28	29	16	9	81	205	217
ANAHEIM	82	29	35	10	8	76	184	213
PHOENIX	82	22	36	18	6	68	188	245

note: Overtime losses (OTL) are worth one point in the standings and are not included in the loss column

CALGARY FLAMES, Player Statistics, 2003-04

#	POS	NAME	GP	G	A	P	Pim
12	RW	Jarome Iginla	81	41	32	73	84
22	C	Craig Conroy	63	8	39	47	44
16	RW	Shean Donovan	82	18	24	42	72
23	LW	Martin Gelinas	76	17	18	35	70
4	D	Jordan Leopold	82	9	24	33	24
37	LW	Dean McAmmond	64	17	13	30	18
18	C	Matthew Lombardi	79	16	13	29	32
19	LW	Oleg Saprykin	69	12	17	29	41
27	F	Steve Reinprecht	44	7	22	29	4
17	RW	Chris Clark	82	10	15	25	106
32	D	Toni Lydman	67	4	16	20	30
28	D	Robyn Regehr	82	4	14	18	74
7	RW	Chuck Kobasew	70	6	11	17	51
11	C	Stephane Yelle	53	4	13	17	24
44	D	Rhett Warrener	77	3	14	17	97
21	D	Andrew Ference	72	4	12	16	53
3	D	Denis Gauthier	80	1	15	16	113
24	F	Ville Nieminen	19	3	5	8	18
26	F	Marcus Nilson	14	5	0	5	14
33	F	Krzysztof Oliwa	65	3	2	5	247
15	LW	Chris Simon	13	3	2	5	25
5	D	Steve Montador	26	1	2	3	50
15	C	Blair Betts	20	1	2	3	10
10	LW	Dave Lowry	18	1	1	2	11
20	LW	Lynn Loyns	12	0	2	2	2
45	C	Jason Morgan	6	0	2	2	2
34	G	Miikka Kiprusoff	38	0	1	1	15
33	G	Jamie McLennan	26	0	1	1	4
1	G	Roman Turek	18	0	1	1	0
50	G	Dany Sabourin	4	0	1	1	0
2	D	Mike Commodore	12	0	0	0	25
25	LW	Martin Sonnenberg	5	0	0	0	2

GOALIES

#		GP	W-L-T	Mins	GA	SO	GAA
34	Miikka Kiprusoff	38	24-10-4	2,301	65	4	1.69
33	Jamie McLennan	26	12-9-3	1,446	53	4	2.20
1	Roman Turek	18	6-11-0	1,031	40	3	2.33
50	Dany Sabourin	4	0-3-0	169	10	0	3.55

All 2004 NHL Playoff Results

CONFERENCE QUARTER-FINALS
EASTERN CONFERENCE

Tampa Bay (1) vs. **New York Islanders** (8)

April 8	Islanders 0 at Tampa Bay 3 [Khabibulin]
April 10	Islanders 3 at Tampa Bay 0 [DiPietro]
April 12	Tampa Bay 3 at Islanders 0 [Khabibulin]
April 14	Tampa Bay 3 at Islanders 0 [Khabibulin]
April 16	Islanders 2 at Tampa Bay 3 (St. Louis 4:07 OT)

Tampa Bay wins best-of-seven 4-1

Boston (2) vs. **Montreal** (7)

April 7	Montreal 0 at Boston 3 [Raycroft]
April 9	Montreal 1 at Boston 2 (Bergeron 1:26 OT)
April 11	Boston 2 at Montreal 3
April 13	Boston 4 at Montreal 3 (Murray 29:27 OT)
April 15	Montreal 5 at Boston 1
April 17	Boston 2 at Montreal 5
April 19	Montreal 2 at Boston 0 [Theodore]

Montreal wins best-of-seven 4-3

Philadelphia (3) vs. **New Jersey** (6)

April 8	New Jersey 2 at Philadelphia 3
April 10	New Jersey 2 at Philadelphia 3
April 12	Philadelphia 2 at New Jersey 4
April 14	Philadelphia 3 at New Jersey 0 [Esche]
April 17	New Jersey 1 at Philadelphia 3

Philadelphia wins best-of-seven 4-1

Toronto (4) vs. **Ottawa** (5)

April 8	Ottawa 4 at Toronto 2
April 10	Ottawa 0 at Toronto 2 [Belfour]
April 12	Toronto 2 at Ottawa 0 [Belfour]
April 14	Toronto 1 at Ottawa 4
April 16	Ottawa 0 at Toronto 2 [Belfour]
April 18	Toronto 1 at Ottawa 2 (Fisher 21:47 OT)
April 20	Ottawa 1 at Toronto 4

Toronto wins best-of-seven 4-3

WESTERN CONFERENCE

Detroit (1) vs. **Nashville** (8)

April 7	Nashville 1 at Detroit 3
April 10	Nashville 1 at Detroit 2
April 11	Detroit 1 at Nashville 3
April 13	Detroit 0 at Nashville 3 [Vokoun]
April 15	Nashville 1 at Detroit 4
April 17	Nashville 0 at Detroit 2 [Joseph]

Detroit wins best-of-seven 4-2

San Jose (2) vs. **St. Louis** (7)

April 8	St. Louis 0 at San Jose 1 (Dimitrakos 9:16 OT) [Nabokov]
April 10	St. Louis 1 at San Jose 3
April 12	San Jose 1 at St. Louis 4
April 13	San Jose 4 at St. Louis 3
April 15	St. Louis 1 at San Jose 3

San Jose wins best-of-seven 4-1

Vancouver (3) vs. **Calgary** (6)

April 7	Calgary 3 at Vancouver 5
April 9	Calgary 2 at Vancouver 1
April 11	Vancouver 2 at Calgary 1
April 13	Vancouver 0 at Calgary 4 [Kiprusoff]
April 15	Calgary 2 at Vancouver 1
April 17	Vancouver 5 at Calgary 4 (Morrison 42:28 OT)
April 19	Calgary 3 at Vancouver 2 (Gelinas 1:25 pp OT)

Calgary wins best-of-seven 4-3

Colorado (4) vs. **Dallas** (5)

April 7	Dallas 1 at Colorado 3
April 9	Dallas 2 at Colorado 5
April 12	Colorado 3 at Dallas 4 (Ott 2:11 OT)
April 14	Colorado 3 at Dallas 2 (Svatos 25:18 OT)
April 17	Dallas 1 at Colorado 5

Colorado wins best-of-seven 4-1

CONFERENCE SEMI-FINALS
EASTERN CONFERENCE

Tampa Bay (1) vs. **Montreal** (7)

April 23	Montreal 0 at Tampa Bay 4 [Khabibulin]
April 25	Montreal 1 at Tampa Bay 3
April 27	Tampa Bay 4 at Montreal 3 (Richards 1:05 OT)
April 29	Tampa Bay 3 at Montreal 1

Tampa Bay wins best-of-seven 4-0

Philadelphia (3) vs. **Toronto** (4)

April 22	Toronto 1 at Philadelphia 3
April 25	Toronto 1 at Philadelphia 2
April 28	Philadelphia 1 at Toronto 4
April 30	Philadelphia 1 at Toronto 3
May 2	Toronto 2 at Philadelphia 7
May 4	Philadelphia 3 at Toronto 2 (Roenick 7:39 OT)

Philadelphia wins best-of-seven 4-2

WESTERN CONFERENCE

Detroit (1) vs. **Calgary** (6)

April 22	Calgary 2 at Detroit 1 (Nilson 2:39 OT)
April 24	Calgary 2 at Detroit 5
April 27	Detroit 2 at Calgary 3
April 29	Detroit 4 at Calgary 2
May 1	Calgary 1 at Detroit 0 (Conroy 16:07 2nd [Kiprusoff]
May 3	Detroit 0 at Calgary 1 (Gelinas 19:13 OT)

Calgary wins best-of-seven 4-2

Colorado (4) vs. **San Jose** (2)

April 22	Colorado 2 at San Jose 5
April 24	Colorado 1 at San Jose 4
April 26	San Jose 1 at Colorado 0 (Damphousse 8:59 3rd) [Nabokov]
April 28	San Jose 0 at Colorado 1 (Sakic 5:15 OT) [Aebischer]
May 1	Colorado 2 at San Jose 1 (Sakic 1:54 OT)
May 4	San Jose 3 at Colorado 1

San Jose wins best-of-seven 4-2

CONFERENCE FINALS
EASTERN CONFERENCE

Tampa Bay (1) vs. **Philadelphia** (3)

May 8	Philadelphia 1 at Tampa Bay 3
May 10	Philadelphia 6 at Tampa Bay 2
May 13	Tampa Bay 4 at Philadelphia 1
May 15	Tampa Bay 2 at Philadelphia 3
May 18	Philadelphia 2 at Tampa Bay 4
May 20	Tampa Bay 4 at Philadelphia 5 (Gagne 18:18 OT)
May 22	Philadelphia 2 at Tampa Bay 1

Tampa Bay wins best-of-seven 4-3

WESTERN CONFERENCE

San Jose (2) vs. **Calgary** (6)

May 9	Calgary 4 at San Jose 3 (Montador 18:43 OT)
May 11	Calgary 4 at San Jose 1
May 13	San Jose 3 at Calgary 0 [Nabokov]
May 16	San Jose 4 at Calgary 2
May 17	Calgary 3 at San Jose 0 [Kiprusoff]
May 19	San Jose 1 at Calgary 3

Calgary wins best-of-seven 4-2

STANLEY CUP FINALS

Calgary vs. **Tampa Bay**

May 25	Calgary 4 at Tampa Bay 1
May 27	Calgary 1 at Tampa Bay 4
May 29	Tampa Bay 0 at Calgary 3
May 31	Tampa Bay 1 at Calgary 0
June 3	Calgary 3 at Tampa Bay 2 (Saprykin 14:40 OT)
June 5	Tampa Bay 3 at Calgary 2 (St. Louis 20:33 OT)
June 7	Calgary 1 at Tampa Bay 2

Tampa Bay wins best-of-seven 4-3

Final Playoff Statistics, CALGARY FLAMES, 2004

FINAL PLAYOFF STATISTICS, CALGARY FLAMES, 2004

#	POS	NAME	GP	G	A	P	Pim
12	RW	Jarome Iginla	26	13	9	22	45
22	C	Craig Conroy	26	6	11	17	12
23	LW	Martin Gelinas	26	8	7	15	35
26	F	Marcus Nilson	26	4	7	11	12
16	RW	Shean Donovan	24	5	5	10	23
4	D	Jordan Leopold	26	0	10	10	6
28	D	Robyn Regehr	26	2	7	9	20
24	F	Ville Nieminen	24	4	4	8	55
15	LW	Chris Simon	16	5	2	7	74
17	RW	Chris Clark	26	3	3	6	30
11	C	Stephane Yelle	23	3	3	6	16
19	LW	Oleg Saprykin	26	3	3	6	14
18	C	Matthew Lombardi	13	1	5	6	4
5	D	Steve Montador	20	1	2	3	6
21	D	Andrew Ference	26	0	3	3	25
33	F	Krzysztof Oliwa	20	2	0	2	6
2	D	Mike Commodore	20	0	2	2	19
7	RW	Chuck Kobasew	26	0	1	1	24
44	D	Rhett Warrener	24	0	1	1	6
3	D	Denis Gauthier	6	0	1	1	4
32	D	Toni Lydman	6	0	1	1	2
34	G	Miikka Kiprusoff	26	0	1	1	0
10	LW	Dave Lowry	10	0	0	0	6
43	D	Brennan Evans	2	0	0	0	0
1	G	Roman Turek	1	0	0	0	0

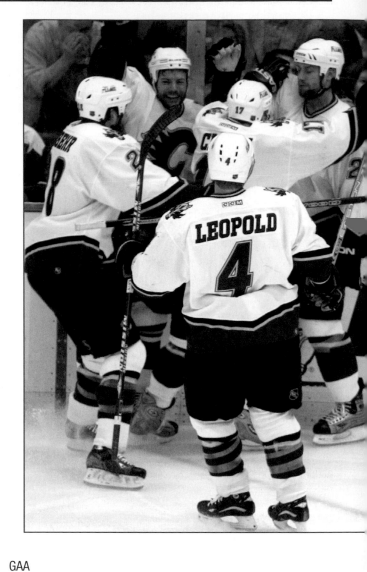

Goalies		GP	W-L	Mins	GA	SO	GAA
34	Miikka Kiprusoff	26	15-11	1,655	51	5	1.85
1	Roman Turek	1	0-0	20	0	0	0.00

How the Team Was Built

BLAIR BETTS
DRAFTED BY Calgary 33rd overall in 1998

CHRIS CLARK
drafted by Calgary 77th overall in 1994

MIKE COMMORDORE
acquired March 11, 2003 with J-F Damphousse from Anaheim for Rob Niedermayer

CRAIG CONROY
acquired on March 13, 2001 from St. Louis with a 7th-round draft choice in 2001 (David Moss) for Cory Stillman

SHEAN DONOVAN
acquired March 11, 2003 from Pittsburgh for Mattias Johansson and Micki DuPont

BRENNAN EVANS
signed as a free agent on September 9, 2003

ANDREW FERENCE
acquired on February 10, 2003 from Pittsburgh for a conditional draft choice

DENIS GAUTHIER
drafted by Calgary 20th overall in 1995

MARTIN GELINAS
signed as a free agent on July 2, 2002

JAROME IGINLA
acquired on December 19, 1995 with Corey Millen from Dallas for Joe Nieuwendyk

MIIKKA KIPRUSOFF
acquired on November 16, 2003 from San Jose for a 2nd-round draft choice in 2005

CHUCK KOBASEW
drafted by Calgary 14th overall in 2001

JORDAN LEOPOLD
acquired on September 26, 2000 from Anaheim for Andrei Nazarov and a 2nd-round draft choice in 2001 (Andrei Taratukhin)

MATTHEW LOMBARDI
drafted 90th overall by Calgary in 2002

DAVE LOWRY
signed as a free agent on July 26, 2000

LYNN LOYNS
acquired on January 9, 2004 from San Jose for future considerations

TONI LYDMAN
drafted 89th overall by Calgary in 1996

DEAN McAMMOND
acquired on March 11, 2003 from Colorado for a 5th-round draft choice in either 2003 or 2004 (Avalanche opted for 2003— selected Mark McCutcheon)

JAMIE McLENNAN
ACQUIRED ON June 22, 2002 from Minnesota for a 9th-round draft choice in 2002 (Mika Hannula)

STEVE MONTADOR
signed as a free agent on September 5, 2000

JASON MORGAN
signed as a free agent on July 11, 2002

VILLE NIEMINEN
acquired on February 24, 2004 from Chicago for Jason Morgan and a conditional draft choice

MARCUS NILSON
acquired on March 8, 2004 from Florida for a 2nd-round draft choice in 2004

KRZYSZTOF OLIWA
signed as a free agent on July 30, 2003

ROBYN REGEHR
acquired on February 28, 1999 with Rene Corbet, Wade Belak, and a 2nd-round draft choice in 2002 (Jarret Stoll) from Colorado for Theo Fleury and Chris Dingman

STEVE REINPRECHT
acquired on July 3, 2003 with Rhett Warrener from Buffalo for Steve Begin and Chris Drury

DANY SABOURIN
drafted 108th overall by Calgary in 1998

OLEG SAPRYKIN
drafted 11th overall by Calgary in 1999

CHRIS SIMON
acquired March 6, 2004 with a 7th-round draft choice in 2004 from Rangers for Jamie McLennan, Blair Betts, and Greg Moore

MARTIN SONNENBERG
signed as a free agent on July 9, 2002

ROMAN TUREK
acquired on June 23, 2001 with a 4th-round draft choice in 2001 (Yegor Shastin) from St. Louis for Fred Brathwaite, Daniel Tkaczuk, Sergei Varlamov, and a 9th-round draft choice in 2001 (Grant Jacobsen)

RHETT WARRENER
acquired on July 3, 2003 with Steve Reinprecht from Buffalo for Steve Begin and Chris Drury

STEPHANE YELLE
acquired on October 1, 2002 with Chris Drury from Colorado for Derek Morris, Dean McAmmond, and Jeff Shantz

WESTERN NHL CONFERENCE

Conference Quarter-Finals
CALGARY FLAMES vs. Vancouver Canucks

Game 1
April 7, 2004
Calgary 3 at **Vancouver 5**

Heading in to the series between these two long-time western foes, much of the talk centred around the absence of Vancouver Canucks forward Todd Bertuzzi, banished for the entire post-season for his late-season hit from behind on Colorado's Steve Moore. One of the things Flames coach Darryl Sutter wanted to avoid was any talk of a letdown with the other team's star player on the sidelines. Even without the 245-pound Bertuzzi in the lineup, the Canucks were a solid all-round team and favoured heading into the series having taken the Northwest Division title by a single point over the Colorado Avalanche.

The home team Canucks rallied for an opening night victory before a sold-out crowd at GM Place, topping the Flames 5-3. Perhaps one of the bigger surprises of the night was that the defensive-minded Flames managed three goals, usually enough for a win thanks to the solid play throughout the season from goalie Miikka Kiprusoff. It almost seemed like it was in the stars that the Flames were meant to win this night. After all, they did score twice on the power play and they also received an even-strength goal from fourth liner Krzysztof Oliwa.

For much of the game, the Flames found themselves on their heels, having to keep the Canucks sharpshooters at bay. But it was special teams that propelled the Canucks to the win. Or, from another perspective, it was a lack of discipline from the Flames that cost them a chance to

Oleg Saprykin beats Dan Cloutier low to the short side to tie the game 2-2 in the second period of game one.

Calgary's Oleg Saprykin whoops it up with teammates Matt Lombardi (middle) and Robyn Regehr (right) after scoring in the second period of game one.

steal game one. The Canucks capitalized by scoring four goals with the man advantage and once with an extra attacker on a delayed penalty.

"I thought our top players had a jittery night", lamented coach Darryl Sutter in a media scrum after the game. "And even at that, we still almost won."

It was apparent that coach Sutter and his staff needed to make it clear to the players the key to winning would be to remain out of the penalty box. When the teams played five-on-five, the Flames more than held their own, and in fact quite often took the play to the Canucks

with the likes of Jarome Iginla and Craig Conroy applying good pressure with strong forechecking deep in the Vancouver zone.

But the Flames were just 2-for-10 on the power play while the Canucks were an impressive 4-for-6.

The fans in Vancouver had lots to cheer about in the early going, as their hometown Canucks built a two-goal lead early when they converted back-to-back Ville Nieminen penalties in the first five minutes on just two shots to forge ahead 2-0.

"We need to get our feet moving. We simply weren't good enough," stated

Calgary captain Jarome Iginla later. Brendan Morrison led the offense for the Canucks with a goal and two assists. Mattias Ohlund notched a goal and an assist while Martin Rucinsky, Sami Salo, and Henrik Sedin also scored for the Canucks. Oleg Saprykin, Chris Simon, and Oliwa replied for Calgary, making a return to the Stanley Cup Playoffs for the first time since suffering a sweep at the hands of the Chicago Blackhawks in the first round in 1996.

Miikka Kiprusoff made 17 saves on 22 shots for the Flames, while Dan Cloutier kicked out 26 shots in the Canucks goal.

Game 2
April 9, 2004
Calgary 2 at Vancouver 1

One thing that could be said for the 2003-04 Calgary Flames is the tremendous resilience they showed throughout the course of the regular season. In fact, following a loss, the Flames had a record of 19-8-4, so the team entered game two at GM Place loaded with confidence they could split the series heading back to Calgary.

The Flames played a far more disciplined game on this night, and coach Darryl Sutter ensured the team played solid, stifling defense. Challenged by their coach to show up, Calgary's stars did just that as the Flames posted a thrilling 2-1 victory in front of 18,630 mostly disappointed Canuck fans at GM Place.

There was no way the Flames wanted to get into another shootout with the Canucks, who simply had too much

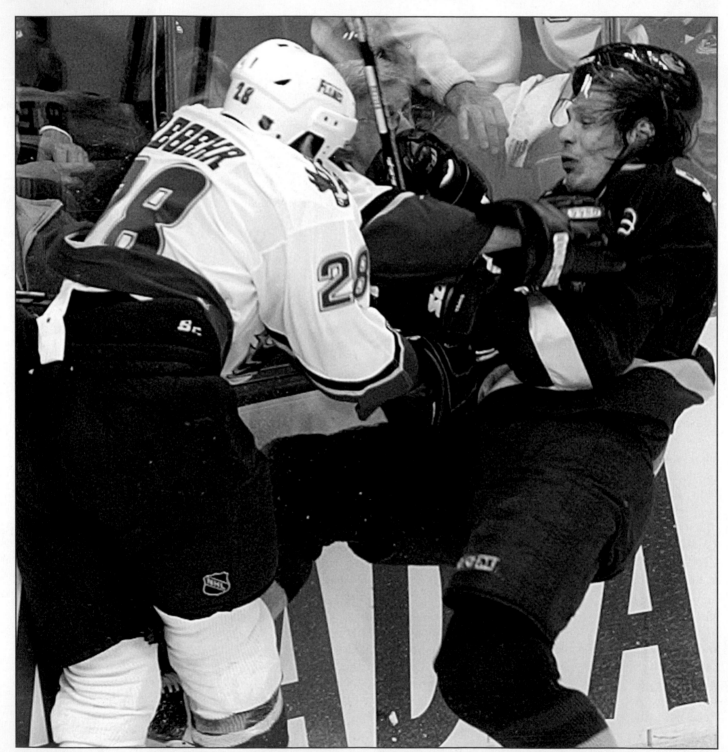

Brent Sopel of Vancouver (right) and Robyn Regehr confront each other behind the goal during the first period of game two.

offensive firepower. It was evident from the first several minutes that Flames goaltender Miikka Kiprusoff was primed for a great game, making several big saves as the team's stars found their legs.

Coach Sutter had demanded more from both Jarome Iginla and Kiprusoff in the Calgary media after the 5-3 loss to open the series, saying if the team was going to achieve any success, they needed to be ready to go when the real season began. True to form, Iginla responded with a dominating effort, crashing and banging in the corners, and setting up numerous scoring opportunities.

"I thought he (Iginla) played with some emotion," Sutter said after the game. "That's important. You have to have emotional leaders."

Iginla and Matthew Lombardi scored 50 seconds apart early in the first period to propel the Calgary Flames to the win. Kiprusoff made 25 saves for Calgary, winners of a playoff game for the first time since 1996.

Markus Naslund scored the only goal for Vancouver, while Dan Cloutier finished with 22 saves in defeat. The Canucks were 4-for-6 on the power play in game one, but managed just one goal on five chances with the extra skater on this night.

"Last game it was all power-play goals," said Kiprusoff after the game. "Today we killed better, and that was the difference."

Iginla scored his first of the playoffs at the 3:06 mark. He had control of the puck behind the net and skated out into the slot, then wristed a shot over Cloutier's glove. Cloutier was out of position on the play, having been bumped by Calgary's big Chris Simon, but the officials interpreted the contact as incidental and not goaltender interference.

Miikka Kiprusoff covers the puck while his defenceman Denis Gauthier eliminates Matt Cooke from the play.

"Simon did a great job of going to the net," Iginla smiled. "I just waited a bit and had a lot of the net to shoot at." Lombardi then scored just 56 seconds later, and that was all the scoring Calgary would need.

Cloutier certainly kept his team in the game by making 12 saves in the second period, but the Flames' solid defense kept Vancouver off the scoresheet as they failed to put any of their eleven shots past Kiprusoff.

After the game coach Sutter also credited the excellent play of some of the younger players on the team, including rookies Lombardi and Chuck Kobasew as well as relative newcomer Oleg Saprykin, who have never faced the pressures of the NHL post-season. It was an especially satisfying win for Lombardi, the hero who scored the game winner.

Calgary was 0-for-5 on the power play after going 2-for-10 in the first game, but the team got the all-important split, heading back to Calgary for games three and four at the Saddledome.

Game 3

April 11, 2004

Vancouver 2 at Calgary 1

The playoff-starved fans of Calgary were in a raucous mood for game three at the Pengrowth Saddledome, their spirits buoyed by the Flames' having split the two games in Vancouver to open the series. Calgary had also not played host to an NHL post-season game since the spring of the 1995-96 campaign.

It was apparent that the Flames would continue to execute a defensive-minded system in an effort to contain the offensive stars on the Canucks. Vancouver deserved plenty of credit for being able to transform their style while at the same time proving they, too, could play strong defensive hockey, limiting the Flames to very few counter-attack chances during the contest. The Canucks played a classic road playoff game, playing a conservative style and not generating many scoring chances, waiting instead to capitalize on Calgary mistakes.

After a scoreless opening period, the Flames hit the scoresheet first when big Chris Simon pounced on a Jarome Iginla rebound to beat Canucks backup goaltender Johan Hedberg. Hedberg had replaced starter Dan Cloutier, who was forced out of the game, and the series, after suffering a knee injury with 29 seconds remaining in the opening period.

Calgary's Jarome Iginla and Vancouver's Mike Keane collide during game three in Calgary.

Canucks defenceman Sami Salo knocks down Martin Gelinas as goalie Johan Hedberg tries to maintain his focus.

It was a rough and tumble affair, typical of games between these two adversaries. Calgary centre Craig Conroy took a high stick from Hedberg and missed a good portion of the second period having his battered face stitched up. But he returned for action in the third, with a full face shield to protect his battle scars.

The Canucks also experienced further injury woes when rugged winger Brad May was forced to leave the game with what was described as "an upper body injury" in the third period.

Just as it seemed the Flames had taken control of the game, the Canucks tied the score just a few minutes later when Markus Naslund tallied on the power play. Matt Cooke's goal created a third period that had Vancouver doing little more than protecting their own zone, refusing to allow the Flames to penetrate and produce scoring opportunities.

A prime opportunity for Calgary to even the score came with 13 minutes to play in the third, when Craig Conroy found himself alone in front of the Vancouver net, but he fanned on an attempted shot. The Flames also had a power play with just over five minutes remaining, but again failed to capitalize. If there was a noticeable weak area for the Flames over the first three games it was the fact they went just 2-for-22 with the man advantage.

Desperate to even the score, the Flames pulled Kiprusoff in favour of an extra attacker hoping to send the game into overtime, but their fate was sealed after an altercation between Canucks defenceman Mattias Ohlund and Jarome Iginla. The Flames captain was hit by a nasty cross check and fell hard into the boards. Iginla was stunned to see no penalty called on the play, and during the heat of the moment retaliated. Both received fighting majors with just eleven seconds left in the third period.

"I thought both teams were great in traffic areas," coach Sutter offered after the game. "It was a night where you earned your ice time."

The loss also extended the Flames home-ice winless streak against the Canucks to 0-8-2, having last beaten Vancouver at the Saddledome on December 29, 2000.

Vancouver defenceman Mattias Ohlund is crushed by two Calgary forwards, Craig Conroy and Jarome Iginla, during game four.

Game 4
April 13, 2004
Vancouver 0 at **Calgary 4**

Once again the Calgary Flames showed why it's tough to beat them two games in a row. Coach Darryl Sutter had the team pumped for game four, and the 18,289 fans made for a dynamic atmosphere inside the Pengrowth Saddledome.

Heading up to the showdown, the Calgary players and coaches admitted that a win in game four was essential. Going down 3-1 in the series and head-ing back to Vancouver would be a daunting task. That negative scenario was certainly not lost on veterans such as Stephane Yelle, who was just return-ing from the injury list. A member of two Stanley Cup winning teams, he was inserted by coach Sutter into the lineup for additional leadership in the dressing room and on the bench.

Following Calgary's 2-1 loss in game three, Sutter challenged his best play-ers to come out in game four and per-form to the best of their abilities. Anything less would jeopardize the season, he said in not so many words.

The players responded in a way Sutter hoped they would. Chris Clark and Shean Donovan pumped in two goals a mere 27 seconds apart, adding to a goal from Yelle earlier in the second period. The Clark goal came about thanks to a horrible line change by the Canucks. Goaltender Miikka Kiprusoff saw an opportunity to get an odd-man rush, and sent the puck hurtling up the ice to Gauthier who then tipped a nice pass on to the stick of Clark. He promptly deposited the puck just under the crossbar at the 16:06 mark. Following the faceoff at centre ice, the Flames immediately

Vancouver defenceman Ed Jovanovski, up on the play, tries to create havoc for Calgary goalie Miikka Kiprusoff.

bore down on the Canucks goal again and with a large crowd seemingly a distraction to Hedberg, Donovan scored, sending the fans into a wild, ear-piercing frenzy as the team built an insurmountable 3-0 lead.

With those three goals, the Flames went into full defensive mode, smothering the Canucks as they entered the neutral zone and chipping the puck out of their own end to take time off the clock. The earlier offensive burst by the Flames clearly deflated the Canucks, who seemed disoriented and unable to establish any form of offensive attack coming out of their own zone. The triumph for the Flames was as much about psychology as anything else. It was the team's first

home victory in the playoffs since Trevor Kidd shut out San Jose 5-0 back on May 15, 1995. It also broke a horrible eleven-game home winless streak against the Canucks.

Vancouver coach Marc Crawford, known for his willingness to gamble and shake things up, attempted to rally his team, pulling Hedberg at various points during the latter stages of the third period in an effort to get on the scoreboard. But even with the extra attacker, the Canucks simply could not muster any offensive power. Adding insult to injury, Jarome Iginla notched his second goal of the playoffs into an empty net at 18:13.

While the Flames netminder Kiprusoff allowed five goals in the

first game of this series, he had now given up only three since. Kiprusoff turned aside all 20 shots he faced, becoming just the fourth goalie in franchise history to record a playoff shutout, joining Mike Vernon, Reggie Lemelin, and Trevor Kidd.

"I thought we played pretty well as a team," Yelle said after the game. "It was a solid, 60-minute effort from everybody."

Sutter was much happier after this game, but remained cautious. "We evened the series up, that's all it was," Sutter said. "It's 2-2 and now is a best-of-three series."

Game 5

April 15, 2004
Calgary 2 at Vancouver 1

The momentum from a strong 4-0 win in game four carried through to game five for the Calgary Flames as they headed to Vancouver. Despite the fact the series was tied 2-2, the Canucks were feeling the pressure to go deep into the playoffs, yet here they were getting all they could handle in the first round. Canucks head coach Marc Crawford was not comfortable with the play of Johan Hedberg in goal. Although he did not blame Hedberg for the game four loss, his subdued verbal support and lack of positive comment on his net-minder's play during press conferences was a strong hint he was thinking about shaking things up for game

five. And that's exactly what Crawford did, opting to insert Alex Auld, who had played admirably throughout the season while Dan Cloutier had been forced to the side-lines with an injury.

Both teams seemed rather tentative in the opening stanza, almost as if it was the first time they'd ever played one another. The Flames opened the scoring in the second period when Auld over-committed on a wide shot by Mike Commodore during a Calgary power play which left Craig Conroy with a wide open net to deposit the puck. The Flames continued to take the play to the Canucks for most of the period but were stymied by some strong defensive work from the Canucks and Auld.

Henrik Sedin tied the contest for Vancouver, which found itself on the brink of first-round playoff elimination for the third time in the last four years. But once again the Flames received leadership from captain Jarome Iginla, who potted the winning goal early in the third period. Iginla also assisted on Conroy's goal.

The Canucks continued to mount offensive chances and nearly tied it when Matt Cooke tipped an Ed Jovanovski shot just wide of the net. Jovanovski also had a great chance in the closing seconds with the goaltender Auld on the bench, but Kiprusoff turned away the point-blank chance from directly in front of the crease.

Flames' goalie Miikka Kiprusoff stones Geoff Sanderson of Vancouver in the first period of game five, won by the Flames, 2-1.

Andrew Ference of Calgary flies past Martin Rucinsky of Vancouver and into the Canucks bench during game five action.

Kiprusoff came up with a plethora of great saves with just over seven minutes left in the period to keep Calgary in front. He stopped a point shot, then turned away Trevor Linden's rebound attempt with a diving stop at the left post. The puck went behind the net and to Henrik Sedin at the right post, but again Kiprusoff slid across the crease to snatch the shot with his glove. Kiprusoff was outstanding between the pipes, kicking out 32 shots in all. Auld finished with 18 saves.

After the game, Canucks head coach Marc Crawford was asked why he decided to switch goaltenders for the pivotal fifth game. "It was a decision on who was going to perform best tonight," he replied. "I thought he was real good. He made some good saves early. It was a tough spot to be in."

But once again the Flames were not taking anything for granted, despite holding a 3-2 series lead going back to the friendly confines of the Saddledome. In the 2003 playoffs, the Canucks came back to win their Conference Quarter-Finals after falling behind 3-1 to St. Louis.

Meanwhile, Calgary had lost in the first round six times in seven years after winning the Stanley Cup in 1989. The club then missed the post-season for seven consecutive years before making the grade once again this spring.

"It's been a tough series," Iginla admitted. "It was a tough game and to be on the verge of winning this series is a great feeling." Iginla had a four-game point streak going, having collected three goals and two assists heading in to game six.

Game 6

April 17, 2004
Vancouver 5 at Calgary 4
(Morrison 42:28 OT)

Fans entering this game on a chilly Saturday night in Calgary probably had no idea they were about to witness one of the most entertaining games in Stanley Cup Playoff history.

The way the game began, there was certainly no reason to believe this would be one of the greatest epic battles the two clubs have ever had. Vancouver bolted out the gate to an early and huge 4-0 lead, only to have the hometown Flames rally to tie before the end of regulation, setting off a marathon overtime session.

It was a bad start which cost the Flames on this night. Calgary showed a lack of discipline in the opening stanza, which led to four separate minor penalties. With the man advantage for a good portion of the period, Vancouver was able to control the tempo, firing the rubber at Miikka Kiprusoff 14 times before finally scoring with just under two minutes left.

Three Flames were out of position when Henrik Sedin spotted a wide-open Jarkko Ruutu unguarded in front of the net who made the easy tap-in for a 1-0 lead. The Canucks then picked up right where they left off in the second period, scoring a pair of quick goals to put the Flames back on their heels. Daniel Sedin tallied his first of the playoffs on the power play 5:32 into the middle period. Just 70 seconds after that, Brad May was also left alone in front of Kiprusoff and he responded with his first marker of the playoffs with a shot that beat Kiprusoff to the stick side.

Fast-skating Geoff Sanderson scored Vancouver's fourth goal. But just when it seemed the most bleak for the Flames, they mounted their extraordi-

Robyn Regehr checks the Canucks' Brad May as the Vancouver forward tries to stuff the puck in the short side on Miikka Kiprusoff during game six.

nary comeback. In fact, it began just 16 seconds after Sanderson's goal.

Oleg Saprykin, Ville Nieminen, Martin Gelinas, and Chris Clark tallied for the Flames during an impressive rally sending the fans into an overtime frenzy.

In the end, it was Brendan Morrison who shattered the party for the 19,289 boisterous Calgarians, who went home wondering if they'd seen their beloved Flames for the last time in these playoffs. The dagger came at 2:28 in triple overtime when Morrison scored, allowing the Canucks to stave off elimination with a dramatic 5-4 win, sending the Western Conference Quarter-Finals series to a seventh and deciding game.

Morrison kept Vancouver's hopes alive by taking a pass from Markus Naslund in the right corner and skating out to the front before going wide to beat Kiprusoff, ending the longest game of the season and longest in Canucks history.

Alex Auld was once again called up to play in goal for the Canucks, stopping 36 shots for the win, including 17 in overtime. Kiprusoff was tremendous in goal, finishing with 47 saves on the first 51 shots he faced, but the 52nd by Morrison proved to be the finishing play.

The Flames had come close to ending the series in the second overtime, but a wrist shot by Ville Nieminen rang off the post after getting by Auld's glove with about eleven minutes left.

The Western Conference Quarter-Finals series now boiled down to a one-game showdown in Vancouver. The Flames were looking to become the first playoff team since the 1985 Minnesota North Stars to overcome a four-goal deficit in one game and claim victory in a series.

Brendan Morrison celebrates his goal in triple overtime as the Canucks stave off elimination and force game seven.

CONFERENCE QUARTER-FINALS — Calgary Flames vs. Vancouver Canucks

69

Game 7

April 19, 2004
Calgary 3 at Vancouver 2
(Gelinas 1:25 OT)

Anticipation of game seven drew to a fever pitch as the Flames and Canucks were set to take the ice, but the first period of this final game was tentative and without incident.

Jarome Iginla ratcheted up his game in the second period when he began to dominate play. The Flames captain got himself open and took a great pass from Craig Conroy and beat Alex Auld for his fourth goal of the series. The Canucks thought they tied the game late in the second when Mike Keane wired a crease shot into Miikka Kiprusoff's pads with the net coming off the moorings. Television replays showed the puck appeared to enter the net before it became dislodged, but officials ruled that the whistle had blown prior to the puck crossing the line.

It was a tough decision for the Canucks to accept, but they kept charging, and it finally paid off with a game-tying marker in the third, off the stick of Matt Cooke, who pounced on a redirected shot off a skate to beat Kiprusoff. A high-sticking double minor was called against Vancouver's Cooke after Rhett Warrener was caught right in the face following a battle for the puck between Cooke and Warrener's defensive partner, Andrew Ference. The Flames took advantage of the power-play opportunity when Iginla recorded his second goal of the night on a nice play set up by Jordan Leopold, who had gone hard to the net up the middle. Iginla deflected Leopold's rebound and smartly deposited the puck around Auld's leg and into the net.

But the division champions from B.C. weren't about to quit. They continued to apply offensive pressure, and the game was in for a wild finish.

Ville Nieminen gets out of the way as Vancouver's Bryan Allen slams into the boards during game seven action.

Calgary's Jarome Iginla beats Alex Auld from in close during third-period action of the deciding game in Vancouver.

Once again it was Cooke who provided the heroics for the Canucks, picking up his second goal of the contest at 12:28 of the third, with assists going to captain Markus Naslund and defenceman Ed Jovanovski.

The two clubs played a scoreless final seven-and-a-half minutes, but the nerves of Canucks fans were frayed when Jovanovski was called for high-sticking with just 27 seconds to play in regulation. Vancouver managed to keep the Flames from scoring, but they still had most of the penalty to kill to start the overtime period.

Overtime in the NHL seems to produce one of two final scripts. Either the game ends in the blink of an eye, or fans can sit back and settle in for a lengthy marathon session. Unfortunately for the Canucks, it all ended very quickly, likely with many fans still standing in the concession lines getting their refills of hot dogs and popcorn.

Martin Gelinas, the 34-year-old grizzled veteran from Shawinigan, Quebec, provided the heroics for the Flames just 1:25 into the extra session, leaving the sellout crowd in GM Place dumbfounded.

To no one's surprise, it was once again the fine hustle of Iginla which led to the game- and series-winning goal for the Flames. Number 12 directed the puck toward the net, Stephane Yelle kept it alive in a scramble, and then Iginla fired yet another shot before Gelinas picked up the rebound and blasted into the net to clinch the series.

Ironically, Gelinas was a member of the 1994 Canucks team that beat the Flames in Calgary in game seven, advancing to the Stanley Cup Finals where they lost to Mark Messier and the New York Rangers in a classic, seven-game series.

Coach Sutter heaped tremendous praise on his captain after the game. "In my 25 years in hockey, that was the single most dominant game I've ever seen a player play," a proud Sutter exclaimed, referring to the three-point performance of his first-year captain, Iginla.

Conference Semi-Finals
CALGARY FLAMES vs. Detroit Red Wings

Detroit's Brendan Shanahan looks for a rebound as Robert Lang beats Miikka Kiprusoff with a shot in the second period. The Flames' Ville Nieminen arrives too late to help.

Game 1
April 22, 2004
Calgary 2 at Detroit 1
(Nilson 2:39 OT)

All the experts in the hockey world were saying that the high-flying Detroit Red Wings would not make an early exit from the Stanley Cup playoffs two years in a row. There was no way the upstart Calgary Flames could match the Wings.

Further, it was expected that the Flames would be easily doused after their emotionally and physically grinding series against the Vancouver Canucks in the epic seven-game series, ending just three days earlier. There was also no way the Flames could play disciplined enough to stay out of the penalty box or be able to fend off the Red Wings and their top-ranked power-play.

It's a good thing the Calgary Flames paid no attention to what the experts had to say! What the experts hadn't predicted was the continued excellent defensive play, stronger goaltending from Miikka Kiprusoff, and even a little lady luck. Not many would dispute the Red Wings held control of the tempo during most of the first game and that the Flames probably stole one at the Joe Louis Arena in a contest that required extra time to decide.

It was an improbable result for the underdogs, who were likely as stunned as anyone in the arena that night. Marcus Nilson scored his first goal of the playoffs, at 2:39 of overtime. He converted a Martin Gelinas pass, making no mistake in finding the top corner with a one-timer and giving Calgary a 1-0 series lead.

"I was screaming at him for the puck," Nilson said after the game. "It was probably luck, but it was nice to see it go in." If the Flames were lacking in confidence heading into the series, that problem was cured after just this one game. It also marked the third consecutive overtime for Calgary and was their fourth win in five games on the road in the playoffs in 2004.

Detroit set the tone for much of the game, but it was the effective counter-attack game-plan by the Flames which worked to perfection. But that perfection may not have looked nearly so good if Kiprusoff had not bailed out his mates on more than one occasion. The Flames mustered just two shots on goal in the opening period, tying a franchise low for a playoff period.

The veteran Wings dominated much of the action during the first 40 minutes and were finally rewarded for their efforts as Robert Lang found the mark at 6:14 of the middle frame.

An emotional boost for the Flames came late in the second at a time they clearly needed a shot in the arm. Detroit had been outshooting them by a margin of 21-9 when defenceman Robyn Regehr cranked a slapshot from the blueline that somehow eluded the mass of players in front of goaltender Curtis Joseph, going into the net at 17:57.

So here they were, badly outplayed over the first two periods against the top team in the NHL during the regu-

Calgary's Ville Nieminen goes to the net and dumps Red Wings defenceman Derian Hatcher into goalie Curtis Joseph in the process.

lar season, tied 1-1 heading in to the third period. It was the just incentive the players needed.

The clubs played to a scoreless tie in the third, setting up sudden-death overtime. In another fast resolution in extra time, Marcus Nilson chose a great time to score his first-ever playoff goal to lift the Flames to a 2-1 victory.

"I didn't really see it," Nilson said of his game-winning shot. "I just heard guys screaming, so I figured it was in the net."

Kiprusoff ended the game with 28 saves. Detroit was a dismal 0-for-6 on the power play. Curtis Joseph made 15 saves at the other end.

"It's a huge win," the winning goaltender agreed. "But that game's behind us and we have to be ready to play the next game."

"We got very lucky," was the honest response from Calgary forward Craig Conroy about the game's outcome. "Now we have to regroup and figure out what we have to do for the first period next game because they came out charging."

Game 2

April 24, 2004
Calgary 2 at **Detroit 5**

It was the plan of the Calgary Flames to try to re-create the same type of game against the Red Wings for game two. Unfortunately, the home side didn't read the script, or, at the very least, demanded a re-write.

Once again the Motor City Red Wings came out on fire, outshooting the Flames 15-3 in the opening period, but the teams went into the dressing room tied 0-0 after 20 minutes. The turning point in the game may have come in that opening frame when Calgary's Rhett Warrener was forced to leave with what appeared to be a serious eye injury. However, he was back on the team bench late in the third period, although by that time, the game was out of reach.

With Calgary minus Denis Gauthier and now Warrener on the defence, Detroit took advantage by hitting the scoreboard first when Tomas Holmstrom deflected a point shot through Miikka Kiprusoff to put the home side up 1-0. Just a few minutes later, the Wings cushioned the lead when captain Steve Yzerman scored his first of two on the night after being left unguarded in front of Kiprusoff. Before the Flames knew what hit them, the Wings had made it 3-0 when Yzerman struck again just 2:13 later, this time leaving defenceman Mike Commodore and Andrew Ference staring at one another trying to figure out how the crafty Wings captain managed to elude them both.

Brett Hull put the Wings up 4-1 when he scored with the Flames down two men on a one-timer through Kiprusoff's legs. The Flames kept it close in the third period, with both

Detroit captain Steve Yzerman beats Miikka Kiprusoff with a high shot to the glove side during the Red Wings' convincing 5-2 win in game two of the series.

teams seemingly resigned to the fact the series would be tied heading out to Calgary.

Calgary captain Jarome Iginla was held without a shot on goal and remained pointless in the series. His frustration showed toward the end of game two when he opted to pick a fight with one of the biggest and toughest Red Wings of them all, 6'5" 240-pound Derian Hatcher. If nothing else, the spirited dustup helped Iginla relieve some of that pent-up frustration and provided the fans at the Joe Louis Arena with a spirited sideshow. Mike

Commodore and Detroit's Darren McCarty also decided to square off in a late-game battle.

Some saw the fighting as a good thing that Iginla showed some emotion and would be fired up for game three. Others said it was merely the superior Red Wings finally wearing down the Flames' star and forcing his frustration to boil over. "He's one of the best players in the world," Joseph said of Iginla. "We have to be aware when he's on the ice."

"We would be happy with a split if we had to get the second game,"

Iginla said following the game. "But in this situation, I don't think we are happy."

Miikka Kiprusoff made 27 saves for the Flames, who were doubled up on shots. "They controlled the puck all night long," lamented Calgary's Craig Conroy. "When they have the puck that much, you're not going to get too many scoring opportunities."

Shean Donovan in the second, and Martin Gelinas late in the third, scored for the Flames.

Martin Gelinas takes his job of crashing the Detroit goal too seriously on this play, knocking into goalie Curtis Joseph as Jiri Fischer looks on.

Game 3

April 27, 2004
Detroit 2 at **Calgary 3**

Fans in Calgary could barely contain their emotion as their Flames headed home to the Saddledome tied 1-1 with the mighty Detroit Red Wings. But with the unpredictable Calgary weather came a wild storm, which somewhat dampened the traditional outdoor parties on game day. Nonetheless, it was a minor inconvenience in the grand scheme of things. A bigger problem came with the news that defenceman Rhett

Warrener would be unavailable to play due to that eye injury suffered in game two in Detroit, leaving the Flames without three of their regular defencemen. In the end, the home boys rallied and skated to an impressive 3-2 win.

Veteran Stephane Yelle turned up his game a notch at another critical time when the Flames needed it most. But it was the Red Wings who opened the scoring early in the second period when Robert Lang collected his own rebound, sending it past Miikka Kiprusoff. It could have been a

momentum shift, but luckily for Calgary, Yelle managed to get the Flames back on even ground, directing a shot past Curtis Joseph through a Chris Clark screen in front.

There was definitely momentum at this stage of the game – and it belonged to Calgary. About two minutes after Yelle's goal, Jarome Iginla was in heavy battle along the boards, had his helmet dislodged, and then converted his first point of the series when he took a Martin Gelinas centring pass and beat Joseph for a nifty power-play marker.

Henrik Zetterberg tries a wraparound that Kiprusoff stops in the third period of Calgary's 3-2 win in game three.

Calgary's Robyn Regehr and Henrik Zetterberg fight for position along the boards.

The Wings tied the game later in the period when Jiri Fischer had a point shot redirect off a Flames defenceman and past Kiprusoff. The Fischer goal brought about an eerie feeling in the building as fans expected an inevitable Detroit surge. But it was the Flames that took control, with Marcus Nilson feeding Shean Donovan to put Calgary ahead to stay at the 12:24 mark of the third. The Red Wings held a territorial advantage in the third period and fired 12 pucks at Kiprusoff, but they were unable to get the equalizer against a determined Calgary defense.

The grit and determination shown by coach Darryl Sutter during his days as a player, and now a coach, was clearly rubbing off on his players. The club had made it through this contest without three of its core defencemen. Detroit was playing without a rather important defenceman as well, with Chris Chelios forced to the sidelines due to an undisclosed injury.

The Flames played a disciplined game, refusing to take senseless penalties, and limiting the Red Wings to just two power-play opportunities, both unsuccessful. As with most playoff series, results often come down to goaltending, and while Curtis Joseph was playing well, Kiprusoff was even better. The Wings had outshot the Flames by a 90-61 margin through the first three games of the series, yet trailed two games to one.

Calgary scored one goal with the extra man this night after going scoreless on eight chances in the first two games.

CONFERENCE SEMI-FINALS — Calgary Flames vs. Detroit Red Wings

77

Ville Nieminen scores on Curtis Joseph to tie the game 2-2 in the second period after the Flames fell behind 2-0.

Game 4
April 29, 2004
Detroit 4 at Calgary 2

If the Pengrowth Saddledome fans seemed wild two nights earlier, they were even louder and crazier on this night as they anticipated the distinct possibility of putting the Presidents' Trophy champions on the ropes, heading back to the Motor City.

But the veteran Red Wings weren't ready to roll over just to make the sellout crowd of 19,289 in Calgary a happy bunch. The Wings scored just 26 seconds into the contest, which quickly transformed the arena from the loudest spot in Canada to a somber den of apprehension. Speedy Kris Draper raced around behind the goal before trying to jam in a wrap-around at the left post. The puck slid

into the slot where Kirk Maltby corralled the loose puck and picked the corner above Kiprusoff's glove hand with a quick shot.

The Flames found themselves down 2-0 after failing to clear the zone, leaving Boyd Devereaux to whistle a screen shot through the legs of Kiprusoff at the three-minute mark. To the credit of the never-say-die

Flames, they came roaring back with a pair of goals 18 seconds apart, which broke a club playoff record set on April 10, 1990, against the Los Angeles Kings when Joel Otto and Paul Ranheim scored 22 seconds apart.

Martin Gelinas benefited from a nice pass out of a scrum in front of Joseph by Jarome Iginla, and the veteran drove the puck into the open net at 5:45. Just 18 seconds later, Ville Nieminen was neatly set up with a pass in front of Joseph and he roofed a backhand just under the crossbar to tie the contest, 2-2.

But the Wings remained patient and eventually received all the breaks they would need, taking advantage of Calgary's defensive errors and hemming the Flames in their own zone for extended periods of time. During one sequence of pressure, Tomas Holmstrom eventually got a shot on Kiprusoff and the puck trickled through the crease onto the waiting stick of Dandeneault halfway through the third period for what was the game-winning goal. Henrik Zetterberg iced the victory with an empty net goal at 19:36.

With the outcome determined, the final seconds of the game were rough and tumble, the main incident coming in the final moments when Nieminen drew a five-minute charging major after skating into Joseph's crease and knocking the goalie into the back of the net.

Detroit outshot the Flames 29-27, Kiprusoff making 25 saves for the Flames. Curtis Joseph, celebrating his 37th birthday, also kicked out 25 shots.

For the time being, the Flames had surrendered that hard-fought home-ice advantage they'd gained against the Wings to start the series. But that pessimism was overcome by the

Henrik Zetterberg battles with Jordan Leopold in front of Miikka Kiprusoff during the first period of game four.

confidence that the team could still pull off a big upset back in Detroit.

Following game four, Calgary had a record of 6-1 in the playoffs when surrendering two or fewer goals, but 0-4 when giving up three or more goals. It was clear to all Flames fans that Miikka Kiprusoff and a stifling defence would be the necessary ingredients for success if they hoped to beat out the powerful Red Wings.

Game 5

May 1, 2004
Calgary 1 at Detroit 0

The Flames went back to the Joe Louis Arena determined to execute their plan of playing a solid defensive game in an attempt to contain the high-flying Red Wings on their home ice. While Calgary did play a strong game in its own end, Detroit was not without its chances to score, totalling 31 shots on Miikka Kiprusoff.

Red Wings defenseman Chris Chelios sat out for the third straight game due to an undisclosed injury. But the big news of the evening was the loss of Steve Yzerman, who was hit in the eye by the puck after it deflected off Rhett Warrener's skate. Ironically, a week ago, it was Yzerman's stick hitting Warrener's eye that sent him to the sidelines. Yzerman was taken to hospital where it was revealed he'd suffered facial fractures around the eye and cheekbone and required about four hours of reconstructive surgery. His playoff run was over.

The game had the potential to be high-scoring, but Kiprusoff was again stellar between the pipes for the Flames. Craig Conroy scored the lone goal of the game at 16:07 of the middle frame, which would eventually propel Calgary to a 1-0 triumph and a 3-2 lead in the series. On the scoring play, Jarome Iginla passed the puck into the slot where Conroy fired it past the glove of Curtis Joseph, who made 20 saves in the Wings net. It was the first time the Wings had been shut out at home in a playoff game in 53 contests, dating back to March 16, 1997, when the St. Louis Blues recorded the doughnut. The goal was also welcome relief for Conroy, who hadn't scored since April 15th.

With a sense of urgency, the Red Wings battled hard in the third period, outshooting the Flames 15-4 over the final 20 minutes, but not all their years of experience and Cup rings and skill could solve Kiprusoff this night.

"We had some opportunities to tie it, but it's a fine line between winning and losing," said Detroit coach Dave Lewis. "They had an opportunity to get the lead, and they got it. We had an opportunity to tie it, but we never tied it."

The Flames got themselves into some penalty trouble in the second period, taking three consecutive minor penalties. "I thought all the

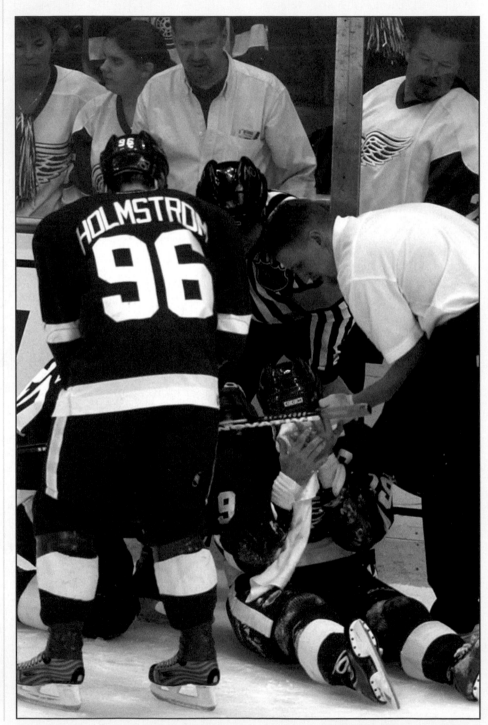

Detroit's Steve Yzerman receives treatment after suffering a serious eye injury from a deflected puck during the second period of game five.

Craig Conroy's shot in the second period in game five proved to be the only goal of the game, and the only one the Flames needed to win this night.

penalties were questionable", coach Darryl Sutter told the media at his press conference after the game.

Great penalty-killing by the likes of rookie Chuck Kobasew, veteran Stephane Yelle, and newcomer Oleg Saprykin helped keep the Red Wings off the scoreboard. In fact, Detroit went 0-for-5 on the power play, although the Flames also failed to score on three chances with the extra attacker.

If there was a troubling habit by the Flames thus far in the playoffs it was an inability to generate fast starts. To this point in the playoffs, Calgary had gone ten straight games without scoring in the first period.

On the brighter side, the Flames played their first hockey game in May since 1989, the year they beat the Montreal Canadiens for their one and only Stanley Cup championship.

Oddly enough, the Flames' biggest wins in club history – a list that includes a Stanley Cup win and an upset over the Edmonton Oilers in 1986 – have all occurred on the road. Some of the players admitted after the game it would be nice to wrap the series up on home ice in game six.

Game 6

May 3, 2004
Detroit 0 at **Calgary 1**
(Gelinas 19:13 OT)

If the mighty Red Wings were going to make a comeback in the series, it would have to be accomplished without the services of their veteran leader Steve Yzerman, out of the lineup after fracturing several facial bones when he was hit by an errant puck in game five.

Nonetheless, it was beginning to look as if Father Time had finally caught up with the aging Wings. Although they played a strong contest this night, facing elimination, the Wings could never shake themselves free of the ambitious Flames, who stuck with them shift-for-shift, refusing to give an inch. Both teams had their share of chances to score during regulation, but after 60 minutes Miikka Kiprusoff and Curtis Joseph remained perfect.

The 19,289 fans in the Saddledome were on the edge of their seats – that is, when they weren't standing and cheering at the top of their lungs. The game, and series, finally came to an exciting conclusion on a play initiated by Jarome Iginla, who had carried the puck from the right corner and fired it toward the Detroit goal. An alert Craig Conroy picked up the rebound and put it back on net, but it hit a skate on the way in and deflected to the far side. As luck would have it, Martin Gelinas was standing there and he made no mistake in depositing the puck into the wide open net, sending the President's Trophy winners on to an early spring vacation. It was his third goal of this series and the fifth goal of the post-season for Gelinas, who also scored the series winner in the first round against Vancouver. And the Wings? Golftown.

"Our team's been resilient," said Gelinas afterward. "I was in the right place at the right time and the rebound came right to me." For Calgary fans, Gelinas is a playoff superhero who was now being aptly called The Eliminator. He became the first player in NHL history to end three series with overtime winners, having also netted the series-winning goal in overtime for Carolina to eliminate the Toronto Maple Leafs in 2002.

Martin Gelinas beats Detroit goalie Curtis Joseph in overtime to eliminate the Wings in game six.

Flames players pour into the corner to congratulate Gelinas on his second successive OT goal to clinch a series.

Iginla had a chance to score the game's first goal in regulation with 9:13 to play, taking a feed at the Detroit blue line and had a shot from the right circle stopped by Joseph. A questionable hooking penalty to Nicklas Lidstrom on the rebound gave the Flames another power play, but they couldn't even muster a shot on goal.

Calgary began to take control early in the contest and almost scored with just over eight minutes left in the opening frame when Iginla rifled a shot into the net from the top of the crease. However, the cage was lifted off its moorings by Kirk Maltby just before the puck crossed the goal line.

Maltby was called for delay of game, but the Red Wings killed off the disadvantage, so the minor penalty, in fact, saved them a goal. The Flames were given another man-advantage moments after Maltby's penalty expired, but again failed to convert.

Calgary won the final two games of the series by 1-0 scores, shutting down the offensive juggernaut that included Brett Hull, Brendan Shanahan, and Robert Lang. It also marked the Flames' first trip to the Conference Finals since 1989.

Last year, much of the blame for Detroit's first-round loss was pinned on goaltender Curtis Joseph, but this

year Cujo was the reason the Wings remained in several games, including game six, when he stopped 43 shots, ten in overtime. Kiprusoff ran his scoreless streak against the Wings to 149 minutes and 11 seconds to close out the series.

"To shut out the Wings back-to-back, he's been awesome," Iginla stated simply after the game.

Calgary improved to 3-1 in overtime this playoff season. The Flames won both overtime games in this series and now were headed to a showdown with San Jose, the winner to advance to the Stanley Cup Finals.

CONFERENCE SEMI-FINALS — Calgary Flames vs. Detroit Red Wings

83

WESTERN NHL CONFERENCE

Conference Finals
CALGARY FLAMES vs. San Jose Sharks

Game 1
May 9, 2004
Calgary 4 at San Jose 3
(Montador 18:43 OT)

The improbable playoff season had now seen the Flames defeat the Northwest Division champion Vancouver Canucks and the President's Trophy winners from Detroit in succession. But another stern test was waiting in the Western Conference Finals against the San Jose Sharks, who had knocked out the Colorado Avalanche in six games. The Flames and Sharks had met once before in the post-season, the Sharks victorious in seven games in the Western Conference Quarter-Finals to conclude the 1994-95 season.

How ironic as well that a San Jose castoff would be one of the main reasons for Calgary's success to this point! Goaltender Miikka Kiprusoff, a third stringer with the Sharks, had become a Vezina Trophy candidate—all within a matter of months.

It was obvious Kiprusoff wanted to prove his former team was wrong in letting him go, and he got off to a great start with an incredible 49-save performance in game one in San Jose, leading the Flames to a 4-3 overtime victory in the opening game.

Through the first rounds of the playoffs against Vancouver, Jarome Iginla was Calgary's best player, but Kiprusoff came up with the timely saves in this series opener.

Since 1989, Calgary had only one overtime win in ten tries but the Flames are now 4-1 in overtime to date in 2004 while the Sharks dropped their third in a row in extra time.

The win was also notable because it was the first time the Flames came

Goalie Miikka Kiprusoff keeps the puck out of his net while defenceman Andrew Ference (right) and Alex Korolyuk (left) of San Jose fight for possession.

The Sharks celebrate Mike Ricci's second-period goal against the Flames in game one, but it came during a 4-3 loss.

out victorious in a game in which they've given up three or more goals. It's no secret Calgary has a much better chance of winning when playing a defensive style, having gone 8-1 when allowing two or fewer goals.

"They are a very fast team, maybe the fastest of the three we've faced in the playoffs," noted Steve Montador, the overtime hero, who scored the winner with just 1:17 to play in the first overtime period. Craig Conroy scored twice and rugged Krzysztof Oliwa also found the net for the Flames.

Even the most dedicated of Flames fans would grudgingly admit they were lucky to come away with a victory in game one. The Sharks controlled the tempo through much of the game and they caught the Flames on numerous bad line

changes, creating odd-man rushes. But luck plus Kiprusoff often equals victory for Calgary.

"We've been able to steal games while they're all over us," said Conroy. "Kipper gave us a chance. We have a whole different kind of confidence with him back there."

Mike Ricci, Todd Harvey, and Alexander Korolyuk replied for the Sharks, who are making their first-ever appearance in the Conference Finals. Evgeni Nabokov, the goal-tending reason that Kiprusoff is in Calgary, was sharp in goal as well, kicking out 33 shots for the Sharks.

On Montador's game-winning goal, Jarome Iginla held the puck in the high slot and waited for Montador to get in position for a good shot. Iginla then fired a great pass right on to the

tape of his stick and he beat Nabokov with a low shot to the stick side.

Just before Montador scored his first goal of the playoffs, Kiprusoff made a pair of great saves on Jonathan Cheechoo.

"It's fun to be here against them (the Sharks), but I don't think it makes any difference," said Kiprusoff. "It's the Finals. That's enough."

Along with Kiprusoff and Conroy, Stephane Yelle also turned in a great game, especially in the defensive zone where he blocked several shots that could easily have led to scoring opportunities for San Jose. Iginla was held in check for most of the contest thanks to some strong blanket coverage from defenceman Scott Hannan, who followed Iginla around the ice with a shadow's consistency.

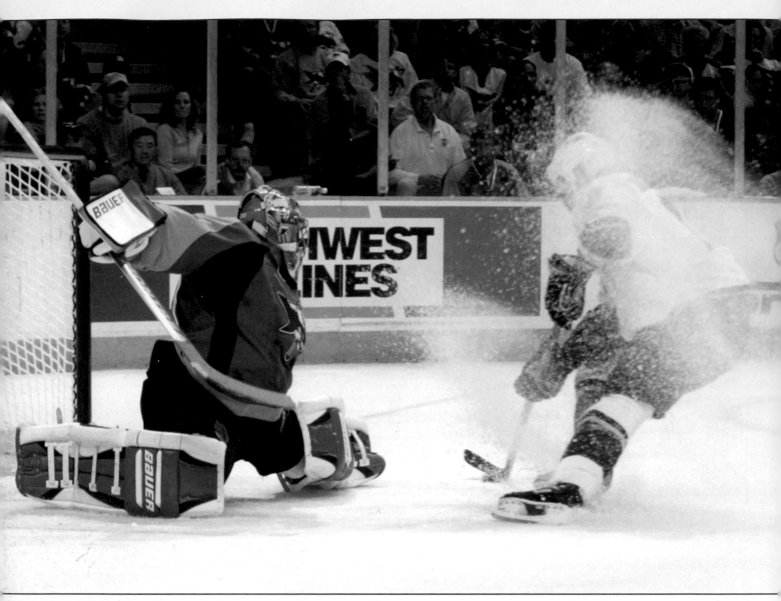

Shean Donovan creates a spray of ice as he beats Nabokov on his first-period breakaway goal.

Game 2
May 11, 2004
Calgary 4 at San Jose 1

Flames coach Darryl Sutter had his team well prepared for game two. One of his greatest worries at this stage was complacency. It was always great to get a split on the road, but that's usually the mindset only after losing the opener. Now the Flames had the chance to take a 2-0 stranglehold in the series. Like Kiprusoff, Sutter also would love nothing better than to defeat his ex-team.

It's almost as if the Sharks were uncertain how to approach game two.

Perhaps it was bewilderment having controlled much of the play in game one, only to come away without a victory.

This was the game the Flames might have been looking for in the opener, showing the Sharks they could skate with them stride for stride, while adding a physical element San Jose might not be able to match.

Shean Donovan, Ville Nieminen, and Marcus Nilson all posted a goal and an assist as the Calgary Flames continued their incredible post-season run with a 4-1 victory. Iginla had the other marker.

The lone goal for San Jose came off the stick of Alyn McCauley. The bad news for Sharks fans is that the club has never managed to rally from down 2-0 in a playoff series in franchise history, and that's exactly where matters stood after this game. The last time the Sharks trailed a series 2-0 was in the 2000 playoffs against Dallas, when they ended up losing in five games.

Calgary entered the third period clinging to a one-goal lead but offered little opportunity for the Sharks to tie it. The best chance for a San Jose equalizer came when Vincent Damphousse nearly swatted the puck into the net when it was hovering about three feet off the ice during a scramble in front of Kiprusoff.

Sharks goalie Evgeni Nabokov looked shaky in the Sharks' net, allowing four goals on just 20 shots.

The game wasn't made any easier for San Jose, playing without rugged defender Kyle McLaren, who was scratched with what was only described as an upper-body injury. Tom Preissing took his place in the lineup.

Regardless, it was textbook Calgary Flames hockey. Playing a controlled, stifling defensive effort, at a high speed, was their motto all season. The Flames provided much tighter checking in this game, never allowing the Sharks to open their offensive game.

"We were a lot better in our zone tonight," said a satisfied coach Darryl Sutter after the game. "I thought our two centremen, Yelle and Nilson, were really good tonight."

It was yet another stellar performance by Miikka Kiprusoff, and the Flames improved their record to 9-1 in the playoffs when allowing two goals or less.

Another reason for coach Sutter to smile was that with the great play of Craig Conroy, linemate to Yelle and Nilson. Their excellent play forced the Sharks to pay more attention to that second line, freeing up Jarome Iginla from what had been double-teaming through most of the first game.

Neither team was able to generate offense with the man advantage, both sides going 0-for-3 on the power play.

The Flames' Chris Simon and Sharks' Mike Ricci collide heavily along the boards during game two.

Game 3

May 13, 2004
San Jose 3 at Calgary 0

By now most of Canada had started to support the Flames for their remarkable playoff run. From coast to coast, the nation adopted the Flames as their own in the hopes they could advance to the Stanley Cup Finals and have the opportunity of becoming the first team since 1993 to bring Lord Stanley back to Canada when the Montreal Canadiens last won. It's hard to believe it was already eleven years ago that the likes of Patrick Roy and John LeClair led the Montreal Canadiens to their triumphant five-game victory over Wayne Gretzky and the Los Angeles Kings.

The sellout crowd for game three at the Saddledome was primed for the game as there was the real possibility that their Flames could take a commanding three-games-to-none lead in the series. There was just one problem. The San Jose Sharks didn't want to co-operate, and instead they skated away with a 3-0 victory to get themselves right back in the series. It also marked the first time in the post-season that the Flames had been shutout.

In what was a very tight game, the Flames were forced to try to open play up in the third period in an attempt to generate the tying goal. But in so doing, they provided more skating room for the freewheeling Sharks, who pumped in two late markers, both by Alex Korolyuk, the second of which was into an empty net.

Goalie Evgeni Nabokov made this save off Martin Gelinas—and all others—shutting out the Flames 3-0 and getting the Sharks back in the series, trailing 2-1.

Ville Nieminen gets too close to Nabokov and pays the price as the equipment-laden goalie falls on top of him.

Coach Darryl Sutter said he knew it would be hard to come back after seeing the Sharks score that opening goal. It meant the Flames needed to abandon their defensive style of play and become more aggressive in trying to get the equalizer.

Make no mistake, though. The Flames had their fair share of early chances to get out in front. In fact, Calgary was outshooting San Jose by a 10-4 margin in the first, but they couldn't get the puck past Evgeni Nabokov, who looked much steadier in goal in this game. He wound up with 34 saves in recording his third shutout of the playoffs.

With the outcome decided, the game turned ugly when the Flames felt that Korolyuk, on his hat trick goal into an empty net, showed the team up. The Russian star stopped and seemed to be showboating before deciding to slap the puck into the yawning cage. The move set off a melee just before the end of the game.

Particularly incensed was rugged Flames winger Chris Simon. Several players began pairing off debating the merits of Korolyuk's actions, grabbing at each other's sweaters. Unfortunately for Sharks defenceman Mike Rathje he met up with Simon in the battles. The two players dropped their gloves and fought, each making a statement to his teammates and opponents alike.

Jarome Iginla was given a game misconduct on the play for refusing to give up his verbal tirade on the officiating. After the game, Flames coach Darryl Sutter said if the club was going to get by this present test and move into the next round of the playoffs, they'd need elevated play from the supporting cast members such as Mike Commodore, Chris Simon, and rookie Chuck Kobasew.

San Jose's Mike Ricci tries to jam the puck in the short side, but goalie Miikka Kiprusoff holds his own and defenceman Rhett Warrener comes in to help.

Game 4
May 16, 2004
San Jose 4 at Calgary 2

During the Stanley Cup Playoffs, fans like nothing more than finding a villain and venting their animosity his way, someone they can latch on to and use as momentum to help propel their team to a higher level.

The villain in this round quickly became Sharks coach Ron Wilson, who drew the wrath of the Calgary fans when he labelled the rabid "C of Red" in Calgary as "nothing special." As several media scribes wrote, it had the potential of being the equivalent of waving the proverbial red flag once too often in the face of the angry bull.

But the Calgary Flames were unable to feast off the wild enthusiasm of the Saddledome fans, giving up a 4-2 loss to the Sharks in game four. The win allowed the Sharks to get back into the series and once again they found themselves with home-ice advantage. Calgary may well have the loudest arenas in the NHL, but it hadn't translated to wins for them in the playoffs as they had mustered only three of eight wins on their own ice in the 2004 post-season.

What seemed to bother coach Darryl Sutter the most after the game was how flat the team appeared at such a critical time in the series. A victory could have given the Flames a commanding 3-1 lead heading back to

California. Instead, it was a best-of-three series now, the teams tied 2-2.

Calgary's Achilles Heel was its failure to produce on the power play. The Flames went just one-for-eight and a rather dismal 2-for-20 overall in the series so far. San Jose, on the other hand, went 2-for-6 with the extra man, exactly the margin of victory tonight.

On this night it was San Jose that provided a stifling defensive effort, limiting Calgary to just 13 shots through two periods. The Flames did generate 16 shots in the third, but it was too little, too late. It was also the first time that Miikka Kiprusoff had lost two consecutive games in the playoffs.

The third period of a rough game saw the Sharks' Brad Stuart manhandled by Calgary's Jarome Iginla and Stephane Yelle.

With the score tied 2-2, Sharks winger Jonathan Cheechoo scored the tie-breaking goal off a Calgary mistake to give San Jose the lead for good.

Mike Rathje, Vincent Damphousse, and Patrick Marleau each finished with a goal and an assist for the Sharks. Evgeni Nabokov made 27 saves in the victory.

Jarome Iginla and Chris Simon scored for Calgary, which fell to 3-5 at the Saddledome in the playoffs.

Miikka Kiprusoff stopped 12 of the 16 shots he faced through two periods before being pulled for the third in favour of Roman Turek, who had a rather easy time, stopping the three shots that came his way as the Flames fought valiantly to get back into the game at the other end of the ice.

If there was a positive for the Flames heading in to game five, it was that their record to this point in the playoffs stood at 7-2 on the road.

This was one of those games when Calgary's better offensive stars were not shining. Among those who did turn in strong efforts for the Flames were Chris Simon, who registered five shots on net, and Stephane Yelle who was consistent and persistent all night long.

Coach Sutter summed up the effort by saying that his players needed to think more about what they were doing, noting the team's mental lapses. "Turnovers cost us the game; no doubt about it," he said after the loss.

Game 5

May 17, 2004
Calgary 3 at San Jose 0

Sharks coach Ron Wilson, hand-picked as the main villain by Flames fans earlier in the series, seemed quite willing to play the part as the series progressed. He was barely able to contain his giddiness after game four, saying it was obvious the momentum had shifted to his team heading back to San Jose. He also relished his team's ability to effectively mute Flames captain Jarome Iginla through much of the first four contests.

However, it was Iginla who scored a goal early after a strong start from the Flames, as they picked off from where they left off in the third period of game four when they outshot San Jose, 16-3. Early in the first period, the Flames generated seven shots on Evgeni Nabokov, while Kiprusoff had seen just one.

Left winger Ville Nieminen showed a lot of grit later in the period when he forced his way in to the Sharks zone after taking a high stick to the throat. A delayed penalty was being called, but in the meantime, Nieminen set up Marcus Nilson with a beautiful pass, and he made no mistake in one-timing the puck past Nabokov for a 2-0 lead.

The Flames put the game away in the second period when hard-working Craig Conroy took advantage of defenceman Kyle McLaren's miscue to score on a two-on-one, using Iginla as a decoy and making the final score 3-0.

A more contrite coach Wilson wasn't nearly as boastful following game five. "We didn't have anyone on the same page, not even in the same chapter of the book."

The Flames are now 8-2 on the road in these playoffs, putting them just two wins short of the NHL record for road wins in playoff season held by the New Jersey Devils of 1995 and 2002. Conversely, though, they are just 3-5 on home ice.

Miikka Kiprusoff made 19 saves for his fourth shutout of the playoffs, tying Tampa's Nikolai Khabibulin for the most in 2004. He also set a Flames record for shutouts, eclipsing the three posted by Mike Vernon in the championship-winning year of 1989.

Craig Conroy spins and fires a shot past Evgeni Nabokov to give the Flames a 3-0 lead in the third period of their win by the same score.

Jarome Iginla finished a long breakaway by stopping directly in front of Evgeni Nabokov and sliding the puck into the open side to give the Flames a critical 1-0 lead in game five.

"We realize how close we are," said Iginla. "It's going to be a tough game six. The two games at home, we weren't that bad... San Jose was very good." Iginla leads all playoff scorers with nine goals and 16 points heading into game six.

It was a doubly sweet day for the Flames' Nilson, who earlier in the day was named to Team Sweden for the World Cup of Hockey.

The Sharks were shut out for the second time in the 2004 playoffs. San Jose has lost four straight home games after winning its first five at the Shark Tank this post-season.

Evgeni Nabokov, who was outstanding in games three and four in Calgary, looked ordinary on this night, making 18 saves.

"Their top line played well in our building; we knew we had to do more tonight," Craig Conroy told the media after the game, referring to the strong offensive performances from Vincent Damphousse, Patrick Marleau, and Alex Korolyuk in game four.

Coach Sutter issued a public challenge to his top players, including Jarome Iginla, Craig Conroy, Martin Gelinas, Robin Regehr, and goal-

tender Miikka Kiprusoff. One and all accepted the challenge, and came through with flying colours.

This series became part of a unique troika in that it is just the third in Stanley Cup Playoff history in which the road team won each of the first five games. It happened in the 1951 Stanley Cup Semi-Finals between Montreal and Detroit and the 1995 Eastern Conference Finals between New Jersey and Philadelphia. A good omen for the Flames: the home club won game six in both previous instances.

Game 6

May 19, 2004
San Jose 1 at **Calgary 3**

At home with a chance to wrap up the Western Conference Finals in front of their own fans. What more could the Calgary Flames desire?

Under normal circumstances, it would be exactly what teams hope for, but given the way their home games had unfolded throughout the post-season, one couldn't blame the Flames if they felt some additional pressure heading in to this all-important game at the Saddledome. While the middling success at home was sure to be in the minds of the players, Sutter told the media before the game he was certain his charges could break free of that mental block.

To inspire his troops, Sutter reminded the players they managed two of three wins on home ice against the league-leading Detroit Red Wings including the clincher in game six, so it was every bit as possible against the Sharks. And to help out, Sutter had his team stay in a downtown hotel to give them a "road game" feeling. It was the veterans who stepped up for the Flames this night, with the likes of Jarome Iginla and Martin Gelinas carrying the team to victory. Amazingly, Gelinas recorded his third consecutive, series-winning goal when he bulged the twine in the second period, en route to a 3-1 triumph and a date in the Stanley Cup Championship Finals for the first time in 15 years. The 26-year-old Iginla notched his 10th goal of the playoffs and fourth of the series.

The Flames jumped out to a 2-0 lead, but the Sharks fought back just over three minutes later when Alyn McCauley's second goal of the post-season found the back of the net. All three San Jose forwards were deep in the zone and the puck eventually found McCauley's stick. With traffic in front, he beat Kiprusoff from the low slot and pulled the Sharks within a goal at 2-1 with 3:46 to go before the second intermission.

The Sharks came out gunning in the third period, directing seven shots on the Calgary goal, but none really tested Kiprusoff, who was able to see all of them clearly. That was what coach Sutter wanted to ensure; that the chances the Sharks got were low percentage shots, keeping the scoring chances to a minimum.

This first-period shot by Calgary captain Jarome Iginla eluded San Jose goalie Evgeni Nabokov and started the Flames on their way to a series victory with the 3-1 win at the Saddledome.

In the final minute, Sharks coach Ron Wilson tried in desperation to generate more offense, pulling Nabokov in favour of an extra attacker with a faceoff deep in the Flames' end. But the Sharks couldn't muster any offense and Robyn Regehr added a last-second empty-net goal with the Sharks storming the Calgary net looking for the tying goal.

"We realized we have the kind of team that can get you a long ways," Gelinas stated. He also scored the series-winning goals against Vancouver and Detroit.

Miikka Kiprusoff, coming off a shutout in game five, allowed just one goal on 19 shots while continuing his stellar play this post-season. Craig Conroy notched two assists. Evgeni Nabokov posted 26 saves for the Sharks in defeat.

"You never know when this opportunity is going to come again in your life," said the always positive captain, Iginla.

Calgary improved to 4-5 at home this post-season heading in to the Stanley Cup Finals but improved to 3-1 with a chance to eliminate a team this playoff season. The only blemish on the team's record came in game six of the opening round against Vancouver. The Flames went 1-for-4 on the power play. The Sharks failed to score with three chances with the man advantage, which was one of the reasons they were headed home.

Iginla, Conroy, Marcus Nilson, Robyn Regehr, Shean Donovan, and goaltender Miikka Kiprusoff played outstanding hockey throughout the series to help put the Flames back into the Finals against the Tampa Bay Lightning, who sent the Philadelphia Flyers packing for the summer in the Eastern Conference Finals. But for the team to achieve the ultimate success of hoisting the Stanley Cup, coach Sutter said that a

The Flames celebrate their empty-net goal at the end of the game which ended a dramatic 3-1 victory to eliminate the Sharks in six games and send the Flames to the Stanley Cup Finals.

few other key players—including Chris Clark, Andrew Ference, and Oleg Saprykin—would need to play

even stronger if the Flames were going to win, such was his confidence in those players.

CALGARY FLAMES vs. Tampa Bay Lightning

Goalie Nikolai Khabibulin, caught out of position, jostles with Calgary's Chris Clark as he scurries back to the goal during third-period action.

Game 1

May 25, 2004
Calgary 4 at Tampa Bay 1

The Flames began the last challenge of their journey with a convincing 4-1 win in Tampa Bay, improving their road record in this year's playoffs to an extraordinary 9-2. The game attracted more than 3 million viewers to *Hockey Night in Canada*, the second-largest audience in the history of the show after game seven of the Vancouver-Rangers Finals in 1994.

It was not the best game of the play-offs, but then again the ice in Tampa was hardly of a quality conducive to speed and skill. Goaltending was one difference in the win—and Jarome Iginla was the other. The Flames quietened the raucous record crowd of 21,674 very early when Andrew Ference flipped a harmless-looking shot on goal. Nikolai Khabibulin was screened, and en route the puck bounced pinball-like off a couple of players in front, Gelinas being the

last, and the puck just slipped between Khabibulin's right pad and the post. Time of the goal, 3:02.

It was just the lucky goal the Flames needed, and it made the Lightning all the more nervous and tentative at a time when they were feeling the pressure of their first appearance of the Stanley Cup Finals to begin with. In the second period, though, they found their legs during the first few minutes and generated some fine scoring chances, but Miikka Kiprusoff was solid in the Calgary goal. As the home side increased the intensity, the Flames responded by matching hit for hit and chance for chance. They played a more physical game than the Bolts, and won most of the battles to the loose puck and the one-on-one fights along the boards.

Captain Jarome Iginla drove a dagger into the hearts of the Lightning during a Tampa power play late in the period when Freddy Modin mishandled a pass and Iginla had a 150-foot breakaway. He shot high, and Khabibulin made a great save, but no one took Iginla and the rebound lay near the crease. He retrieved the loose puck—Khabibulin didn't know where it was—and slid it hard into the open side to give the Flames a solid 2-0 lead.

Less than three minutes later, Stephane Yelle sealed the game when he came out from behind the net, faked a wraparound shot, stopped, and roofed the puck in the short side with Khabibulin on his knees, stick along the ice. Martin St. Louis scored in the third for the Lightning at 4:13 on the power play, but the goal didn't ignite his team and the Flames didn't panic at the prospects of a comeback by the home side.

Kiprusoff outplayed Khabibulin, to be sure, but Iginla played like a man on a mission, driving to the net, finishing his checks, and creating scoring chances out of harmless-looking situations. The Flames pounded the mobile Tampa defence all night, ensuring the defencemen wouldn't join the rush the way they had done so successfully in these playoffs through the first three rounds. And, the battle between Calgary's superb penalty killing and Tampa's awesome power play was won by the Flames' defence which allowed just the one Martin St. Louis goal on six man-short situations.

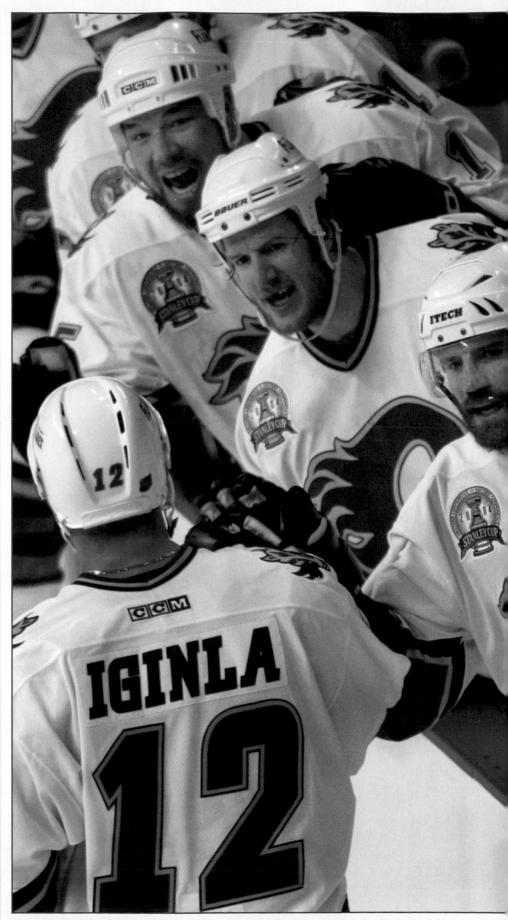

Jarome Iginla receives high-fives from the bench after scoring in the second period to give the Flames a 1-0 lead in game one of the Stanley Cup Finals.

Game 2

May 27, 2004
Calgary 1 at **Tampa Bay 4**

The Lightning did what they had done all playoffs: follow a loss with a win. And, none was bigger than this 4-1 victory to get back into the series, tied 1-1 now heading to Calgary for games three and four. All the big guns had a hand in the win for Tampa Bay: Vincent Lecavalier was dominating; Brad Richards scored another game winner; Martin St. Louis scored the back-breaker; and, goalie Nikolai Khabibulin was rock solid in the nets.

It all started with Lecavalier. Behind the Calgary net early in the first period, he beat a Flames defenceman by banking the puck off the back of the net, twirling out of the way, and regaining the puck. He moved to the side boards, made a lovely cross-ice pass to Jassen Cullimore, who took a quick shot on goal. Miikka Kiprusoff made the save, but before he could get the rebound Ruslan Fedotenko swiped it in for his 10th goal of the playoffs to give Tampa a 1-0 lead.

But the Flames had chance after chance on the power play and couldn't tie the game or generate scoring

opportunities to give themselves confidence or momentum. They were hesitant moving the puck out of their end with the man advantage and never maintained control of play in the Lightning end. As the power play dwindled, so did their chances of winning.

Yet by the start of the third period the Flames were still only a shot away from tying the game. They killed off a 45-second 5-on-3 chance by Tampa, but instead of building on this they were burned when Brad Richards scored when he one-timed a loose puck with a perfect shot off the

Martin St. Louis of Tampa looks for a loose puck while Calgary goalie Miikka Kiprusoff looks on anxiously. The Lightning won 4-1 to tie the series 1-1.

far post. Just 69 seconds later, Dan Boyle, off a lovely pass from Richards, made it 3-0, and the game was, for all intents and purposes, over. Martin St. Louis made it 4-0 at 5:58 on another 5-on-3 chance, and the Flames' Ville Nieminen scored his team's only goal midway through the period, also on the power play. Too little, too late.

Calgary went 1-for-7 on the power play and the Lightning 1-for-8, and although neither team was particularly effective with the extra man (in the sense that special teams didn't decide the outcome), all the odd-man play over the course of the game certainly helped the smaller, quicker Lightning.

It was an odd situation this night as Lecavalier and Richards played their best games. In the stands was none other than Wayne Gretzky, manager of Canada's World Cup entry this August. He watched as one of his selections, Richards, tied an NHL record, while one player he didn't choose—Lecavalier—had an equally outstanding game!

For Richards, it was his sixth game-winning goal of these 2004 playoffs, tying the NHL record held by Joe Nieuwendyk (1999) and Joe Sakic (1996). For the Lightning, it meant the team had now evened the series 1-1 and had as much a chance to win the Stanley Cup as their opponents.

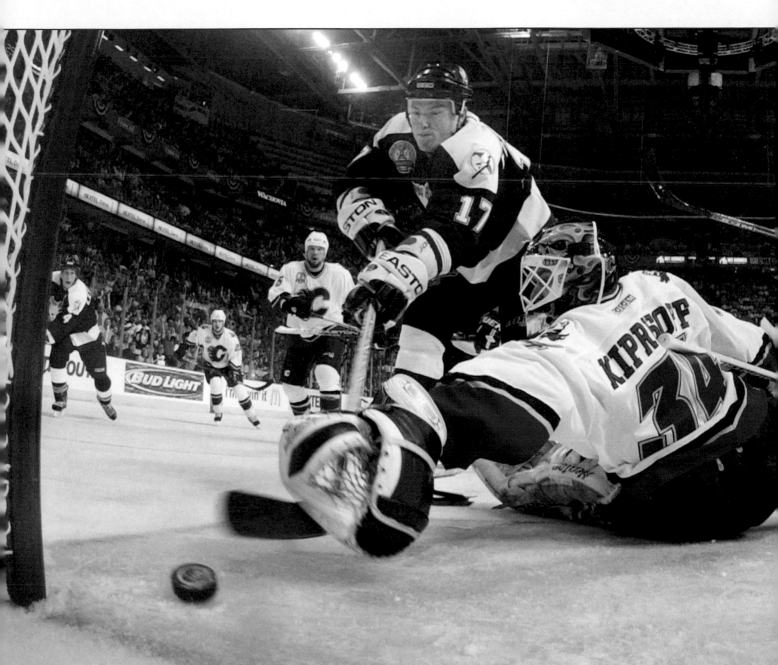

Tampa Bay's Ruslan Fedotenko gets to the loose puck before goalie Kiprusoff can get to it. The goal gave the Lightning a 1-0 lead in the first period and they went on to win 4-1.

Game 3

May 29, 2004
Tampa Bay 0 at Calgary 3

Perhaps never before has the hockey adage been so applicable as this night, when the Lightning failed to score at one end of the ice and the Flames scored on the ensuing rush the other way.

It was this simple: In a tentative game that was still scoreless midway through the second period, the Flames were on the power play after Brad Lukowich of Tampa Bay took a slashing penalty at 13:03. This seemed to be of little matter, because no matter how amazing the Flames have been this playoffs, their power play has been ineffective. Vincent Lecavalier stole the puck just inside his blueline and saw a streaking Brad Richards up ahead. He hit him with a perfect pass, Flames defenceman

Robyn Regehr in hot pursuit, and Richards got off an excellent shot from the right wing, his off-wing. But there in goal was Miikka Kiprusoff, who got his blocker on the drive to keep the game scoreless.

Play moved up ice, Jarome Iginla taking the puck deep into the Tampa end where he passed to Chris Simon. The hulking Simon had three whacks at the puck, the third one, from the side of the net, eluding Nikolai Khabibulin and finding the back of the goal. The Flames took a 1-0 lead; they had scored with a power play; and the 19,221 fans at the Saddledome went berserk.

Less than four minutes later, Shean Donovon was on his off wing, barreling down the left side on a two-on-one. He couldn't make the pass across, so instead shot high over Khabibulin's glove, off the crossbar,

and down into the goal. Two quick strikes, and the Flames had what turned out to be an insurmountable lead of 2-0 by the end of the second period. Jarome Iginla added a late score in the third period—also on the power play—and the Flames' 3-0 win gave them a 2-1 lead in the series for Lord Stanley's Cup.

Although the two teams entered this Finals as exciting, offensively capable teams, their inexperience and nervousness of competing for a prize they never thought possible at the start of the year resulted in cautious, defensive play. First period shots in game three were just 5-2 for Tampa Bay, but ask any player in the Calgary dressing room and he'd say the turning point came in that first, tenuous 20 minutes, when Iginla and Lightning star Vincent Lecavalier got into a fight. Iginla became a different man after the fight, while Lecavalier

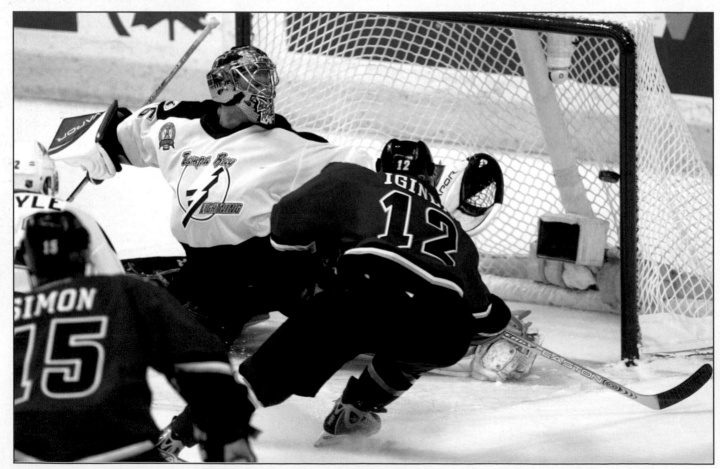

Jarome Iginla scores on a power play in the final minutes in game three, putting the finishing touches on a superb 3-0 victory for the Flames.

Chris Simon jumps into the boards in celebration after scoring the opening goal of game three, in the second period on the power play, to lead the Flames to victory.

disappeared into the ether the rest of the night. In all, Iginla had the proverbial Gordie Howe hat trick, starting with the fight, continuing with the assist on Simon's goal, and completing the trick with his own goal in the third.

The Flames proved once again how critical the first goal of the game is to both teams. They are now 12-1 when scoring first, and the Lightning are 11-2 when doing so. Although the game is 60 minutes long, it seems as though 'first goal wins' is the rule of the playoffs for these two teams.

The Flames played near perfect defence all night, surrendering just 21 shots. Kiprusoff, Richards break-away aside, was great when he had to be, but he wasn't as severely tested as he was in game two when he allowed four goals. But again, he proved his ability to bounce back after a loss. In these 2004 playoffs, his record is 7-1 in games following a loss. The Flames were now in a position to take a stranglehold on the series if they were to win game four, also at home, two nights later.

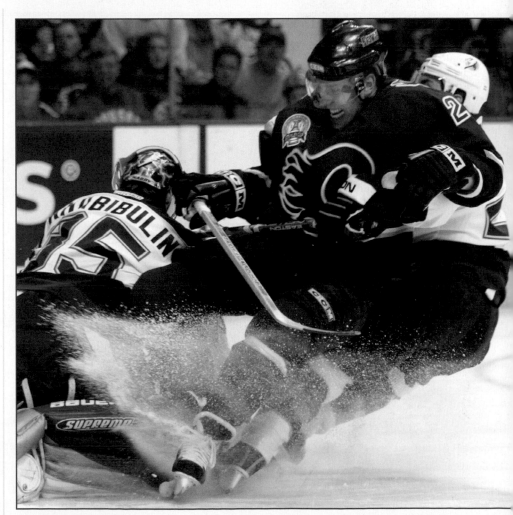

Tampa Bay goalie Nikolai Khabibulin holds his ground to make a save while Calgary's Ville Nieminen is guarded closely by defenceman Dan Boyle.

Game 4
May 31, 2004
Tampa Bay 1 at Calgary 0

The consistency of play for both Tampa Bay and Calgary has been so impeccable that determining the outcome of a game seems to come down not to play or breaks but simple percentages. When Tampa Bay scored early in the game this night, the team virtually assured itself of victory, especially since Brad Richards was the goal scorer. The Lightning had an incredible record of 22-0-2 during the regular season in games in which Richards scored a goal, and in the playoffs that unbeaten streak was a

perfect 7-0. After game four, make it 8-0. The Lightning are now 12-2 in games they score the first goal, and the Flames' home woes continue.

Flames fans, though, have a new skater to hate, and he doesn't play for Tampa or any previous team. No, it's referee Kerry Fraser who called Chris Clark for cross checking at 1:52 while the other referee, Brad Watson, called Mike Commodore for holding. As a result, the Lightning had a two-minute power play 5-on-3 in the second minute of the game, and when Richards wired a shot past the outstretched glove of Miikka Kiprusoff at 2:48, he gave his team all it would

need to tie the best-of-seven Finals 2-2 and reclaim home-ice advantage heading back to Florida for game five. It was Richards' seventh game winner this year, an NHL record.

That the Lightning won without their best defenceman, Pavel Kubina (concussion) and leading goal scorer (Ruslan Fedotenko, with ten goals) is testament to the effectiveness of their team play. That they came out and matched the physical play of the Flames hit for hit and then preserved a lead for 57 minutes is also testament to their play without the puck and their ability to play defensive hockey when they have to. This was

Brad Richards' point shot beats Miikka Kiprusoff during a 5-on-3 power play for the Lightning early in the game, a goal that stood as the game winner.

Soon after Tampa Bay took a 1-0 lead, Calgary's Jarome Iginla had a good chance to tie the game, but he was bested by Lightning goalie Nikolai Khabibulin on the play.

no great game to watch, but for Tampa, the players got the job done.

Even more amazing was the fact that the Flames had only two power plays all night, both in the first period, and although they had good pressure and created a few chances, they didn't convert on either and the Lightning did a good job of staying out of the box the rest of the game. The same can't be said for Ville Nieminen who hit Vincent Lecavalier from behind along the glass at centre ice late in the third period and received a five-minute major and game misconduct. Lecavalier suffered a cut to his head, and although he didn't leave the bench,

coach John Tortorella wisely kept him off the ice the rest of the game.

The Flames started the second period with close to two solid minutes of pressure in the Lightning end, but their quality chances were few and far between and goalie Nikolai Khabibulin was rock solid when challenged. In fact, some of Calgary's best chances came when they were short-handed, but overall they lacked the killer instinct that they brought to the Saddledome for game three.

Tampa Bay played a perfect road game, not trying to do anything fancy, knocking the puck off the glass

and down the ice whenever they were pressured or didn't have an open man. Calgary often initiated the hitting in the game, and since this is now going to be a long series it might have an effect in the last three games, but the physical play didn't establish momentum or give them an advantage this night as it had in game three.

And so now the Flames head back to the road where they have such an incredible record in the 2004 play-offs, realizing that if they are to win the Stanley Cup, they'll have to win two of the next three games, at least one of which will have to come in Tampa Bay.

Game 5

June 3, 2004
Calgary 3 at Tampa Bay 2
(Saprykin 14:40 OT)

It was the most thrilling game of this year's Cup Finals to date, a game that featured goals and momentum swings, phenomenal speed and end-to-end rushes, but when Oleg Saprykin finally scored the winner for Calgary at 14:40 of the first overtime period, justice had been done and the better team had won.

Something had to give on this night for the crucial game five. Both teams had a combined 6-0 record in game fives so far in these playoffs, testament to their ability to win the pivotal game.

Typical for the Flames, they played an incredible road game. They came out on the attack, and this time it was they who got the early power play and scored. Fredrik Modin was called for a high stick, and on the ensuing power play the visitors made

Tampa Bay pay. Defenceman Toni Lydman, in the game in place of Mike Commodore, took a quick but innocent-looking snapshot on goal, and Martin Gelinas deflected the puck through the legs of Nikolai Khabibulin and into the net at 2:13 for an early 1-0 Calgary lead.

The Flames are 12-1 this year when scoring first, but tonight that stat didn't mean much. The Flames dominated the rest of the period but could not get that second, back-breaking goal. Instead, the Lightning tied the game in the period's final minute when the relentless Martin St. Louis bulldozed his way from behind the net out front and took a backhand shot that handcuffed Miikka Kiprusoff in the Calgary goal and trickled over the goal line.

The goal gave the Lightning life when they had no business being in the game, but the resilient Flames came out to start the second period just as they had the first, seemingly unaffected by the disappointing tying goal by

St. Louis. Again, they were rewarded. Captain Jarome Iginla drove down the right wing and blasted a slapshot that caromed off the far post and in, giving the Flames a 2-1 lead. This time, there was no letdown, and after 40 minutes that's how the score stood.

Early in the third, though, there was another change in momentum when Rhett Warrener was called just 31 seconds into the period for holding the stick. A mere six seconds later, Brad Richards feathered a beautiful pass to Modin alone in front, and he directed the puck between Kiprusoff's legs in the blink of an eye to tie the game, 2-2. The rest of the period was thrilling hockey. There was no sitting on the lead, no cautious play, no trap. Teams went end-to-end, shift after shift, wave after wave. Bodies flew everywhere from hard, clean hits, and both goalies made excellent saves when called upon. It was obvious that the next goal was going to be the winner, and after 60 minutes that fact was confirmed when teams went to overtime for the first time in this series.

Amazingly, the overtime resembled open-ice shinny as much as a period upon which the Stanley Cup might well be decided. Both teams wanted to score, and the best way to do that was attack. More end-to-end action followed, and both teams had plenty of chances to score. The turning point came on the best individual shift of the night by anyone on the ice, when Iginla dominated play in the Tampa Bay end for what seemed like a minute.

Early in the shift he lost his helmet on a hit behind the Lightning goal, and when the puck came back in the Tampa end he was a one-man forechecking crew. The puck came loose to the side of the goal. Iginla, with his back to Khabibulin, controlled the puck, spun, and drilled a shot to the chest of the goalie.

Martin St. Louis ties the game 1-1 for Tampa Bay with this backhand shot that eludes goalie Miikka Kiprusoff in the final minute of the first period.

Khabibulin made the stop, but the puck fell to the ice and Oleg Saprykin knocked the rebound through the goalie's legs to empty the Flames bench and send them back to Calgary with a chance to win the Stanley Cup.

Back home at the Pengrowth Saddledome, a sold out crowd cheered wildly while watching the game on the big screen above centre ice, their heroes a few thousand kilometres away.

With the victory Calgary tied New Jersey for most road wins in a playoff year (10), a record the Devils set in 1995 and again in 2000. They won the Cup each year.

Flames players roar off the bench to leap on their overtime hero, Oleg Saprykin, whose goal put his team one win away from a remarkable Stanley Cup victory.

Oleg Saprykin jumps on a loose puck and slides it underneath goalie Nikolai Khabibulin at 14:40 of overtime to give the Flames a well-deserved 3-2 win and a 3-2 series lead heading home to Calgary with a chance to clinch the Cup.

Game 6

June 5, 2004
Tampa Bay 3 at Calgary 2
(St. Louis 20:33 OT)

In a game six that mirrored the previous meeting in this series, Tampa Bay silenced the wild hometown Calgary crowd with a stunning 3-2 victory to force game seven and force the Hockey Hall of Fame staff to pack up the Stanley Cup that was ready to go onto the ice at the Pengrowth Saddledome had the Flames won.

Martin St. Louis was the hero for the Lightning, lifting a rebound high over goalie Miikka Kiprusoff after he stopped a weak point shot from Tim Taylor at the Calgary blueline early in the second overtime period. The dramatic goal kept alive a most extraordinary streak in that Brad Richards scored twice for the visitors tonight, giving his team a perfect 9-0 playoff record when he scores a goal.

As in game five, the visiting team went up 1-0 and 2-1, only to be tied in each instance. Both of Richards' goals in regulation came on the power play. After a scoreless first period in which Calgary looked nervous and Tampa Bay ineffective, the Lightning got a power play after killing off two, man-short situations of their own. With Jordan Leopold in the penalty box, Tampa Bay moved the puck around in the Calgary end with confidence, although Richards' goal was hardly a work of beauty. Standing in the corner, on the goal line, he drilled a shot through the crease. Kiprusoff went down and tried to deflect the puck out of harm's way, but in the process knocked it into his own goal to give the Lightning a 1-0 lead at 4:17.

The first goal, which had been so vital in the first four games, was not so special in game five or on this night, either. The Flames reacted by storming the Tampa defence. Five minutes later, Ville Nieminen whipped the puck through the crease while down on one knee, and Chris Clark took the back-door pass and slammed it into the empty side to tie the game, 1-1.

Chris Clark bangs in a beautiful cross-crease pass from Ville Nieminen that eluded two Tampa Bay players. The goal tied the game, 1-1.

Calgary's Marcus Nilson celebrates his game-tying goal late in the second period after a lovely pass by Oleg Saprykin that left goalie Nikolai Khabibulin at the shooter's mercy.

The rest of the period was all Calgary, as was most of the third, but no matter how much they pressed the Flames couldn't score the go-ahead goal, the Cup-winning goal. In the first overtime, the Lightning had the better of the play for the first half but sagged noticeably. Again, all the pressure in the world couldn't get the Flames that winning goal and a second OT resulted. Less than a minute into that fifth period, St. Louis saved the day for Tampa Bay and forced a game seven with his 9th goal of the playoffs to send the disappointed crowd of 19,221 into the Red Mile Calgary night without a Stanley Cup party to enjoy.

Incredibly, the Flames now have a 5-7 home record during these playoffs and are 10-3 away from the Saddledome. If they win game seven, they'll be the first team in Cup history to win with a losing home record.

Just 20 seconds later, though, the Flames' Craig Conroy was called for hooking, and the visitors were right back on the power play. Again, they controlled the puck beautifully in the Calgary end. Again it was Richards doing the damage, this time by recovering a loose puck in the slot and ripping a low shot through Miikka Kiprusoff's legs to give the Lightning a 2-1 lead.

Late in the period, Calgary tried a routine dump-in and came up short, but Tampa defenceman Dan Boyle mishandled the puck, giving Calgary a quick 2-on-1 on the turnover. Oleg Saprykin carried the puck toward the goal, waited for the defenceman to commit, and fired a perfect pass to Marcus Nilson who simply put his stick down and directed it in to tie the game again, 2-2.

Tampa Bay's superstar forward Martin St. Louis lifts the puck over Miikka Kiprusoff's shoulder just 33 seconds into the second overtime period to give the Lightning a 3-2 win and send the series back to Florida for one final game, the winner to claim the Stanley Cup.

Ruslan Fedotenko finishes a lovely play, taking Vincent Lecavalier's brilliant pass from the corner and drilling a shot past the outstretched glove of Miikka Kiprusoff.

Game 7
June 7, 2004
Calgary 1 at **Tampa Bay 2**

The Tampa Bay Lightning put the finishing touches on their dream season by ending the dream run of the Calgary Flames, defeating Calgary 2-1 in a dramatic, nail-biting game seven to win the Stanley Cup. It was a game in which Tampa's team speed finally proved superior to the Calgary defense as it generated numerous scoring chances while preventing much in the way of offense from the Flames.

The Flames were on the defensive almost from the opening faceoff when Marcus Nilson was called for slashing at 1:10. As a result, they had to kill a penalty before they had a chance to establish their own game of skating, forechecking, and hitting.

Although the Flames survived that early penalty, they weren't so fortunate later in the period when Oleg Saprykin was in the penalty box. Once again, Brad Richards quarterbacked the Lightning power play from the point, and as he does so well he took a simple wrist shot toward the goal before it could be blocked. Goalie Miikka Kiprusoff made the save, but Ruslan Fedotenko swept the rebound between the goalie's legs at 13:31 for the game's opening goal. It marked the 12th time in the past 13 games that the Lightning had scored at least one power-play goal and, in the end, meant Tampa had a 14-2 record this playoffs when scoring first.

The goal ignited the Lightning more than the Flames and just a few moments later a defensive lapse by Calgary allowed defenceman Dan Boyle to sneak in from the point and take a pass in the slot from Freddy Modin. Boyle hit the post, but the rest of the period belonged to Tampa Bay.

The Lightning didn't let up in the second period and the Flames couldn't find their game. Calgary had an early power play but could do little with the extra man, and later in the period Vincent Lecavalier made the play of the game. Deep in the Calgary zone, he twisted and twirled, cycled and deked by himself for about ten seconds, mesmerizing the Flames and then threading a lovely pass to Fedotenko alone in the slot. He drilled a high shot over Kiprusoff's glove for his second goal of the game at 14:38 to give the Lightning a commanding 2-0 lead.

A dejected Calgary Flames bench reacts to Ruslan Fedotenko's second goal of the game to give Tampa Bay a 2-0 lead.

For the rest of the second period and half of the third, Tampa Bay played precise defensive hockey, allowing few chances by the Flames and blocking shots as if every man on the ice were a goalie. Calgary got only its second power play of the night midway through the final period, though, and a Craig Conroy point shot beat Nikolai Khabibulin over the glove to make it 2-1. Thus started the most frenzied ten minutes of the playoffs as the Flames sent wave after wave into the Tampa Bay zone, coming close many times but failing to tie the game.

Their best chance came when Jordan Leopold had half an open net when Khabibulin made a great pad save but kicked the rebound to the Calgary defenceman. But as Leopold shot, Khabibulin did the splits and took away a sure goal with a remarkable blocker save.

The Flames didn't get Kiprusoff to the bench for any length of time and the Lightning weathered the storm to win their first Stanley Cup. For the Flames, the loss ended an incredible season, a dream season, a playoff run that nobody expected but one that in the end enthralled not only a city and province, but an entire country. The Calgary Flames may have lost the Stanley Cup, but they made millions of fans across Canada.

After more than 1,700 NHL games, 40-year-old Dave Andreychuk holds the Stanley Cup for the first time.

Recalling the 1988–89 Calgary Flames

The on-ice team portrait the night of May 25, 1989, at the Forum in Montreal.

Game 1

May 14, 1989
Montreal 2 at **Calgary 3**

The Canadiens got an early power-play goal when Stephane Richer scored with Jim Peplinski in the penalty box, but two goals from defenceman Al MacInnis gave the Flames a lead. It was short-lived, though, as Larry Robinson tied the game two minutes later. Theo Fleury scored the game winner midway through the second period, and goalie Mike Vernon kept the Habs off the scoresheet the last 50 minutes to preserve the victory.

Game 2

May 17, 1989
Montreal 4 at Calgary 2

Larry Robinson scored the only goal of the first period, and when Steve Smith scored on the power play just 1:55 into the second the Canadiens had a healthy 2-0 lead. Joe Nieuwendyk got the Flames going a few minutes later, and Joel Otto tied the game for the home side later in the period, but two third-period goals by the Habs salted the victory and Montreal headed home with a split in the series.

Game 3

May 19, 1989
Calgary 3 at **Montreal 4**
(Walter 38:08 OT)

In what was a heart-breaking loss for the visiting Flames, Montreal withstood an early barrage by Calgary and won a thriller late in the second overtime period on a goal by Ryan Walter. The Habs scored first, Mike McPhee doing the honours just 1:32 in the game. Then Patrick Roy took over and stopped 12 of 13 shots he faced in the period (Montreal had but four). Joe Mullen scored late to send the teams to the dressing room tied

1-1, and he scored the only goal of the second period as well. Bobby Smith tied the game again for Montreal in the third, and for the second time the Flames took the lead, this time thanks to a goal by Doug Gilmour at 13:02. The Habs tied the game 3-3 with just 41 seconds left in regulation time, a Mats Naslund shot beating Mike Vernon and deflating the Flames. In the first overtime, there was an amazing four sets of coincidental minors called by referee Kerry Fraser in a game that had been penalty filled from the start. Walter's OT winner was scored at 18:08, the same time a two-minute minor to Mark Hunter expired.

Game 4
May 21, 1989
Calgary 4 at Montreal 2

Showing remarkable resilience, the Flames bounced back from their emotionally exhausting defeat to tie the series and re-claim home-ice advantage. Although the first period was scoreless, they outshot the home side 13-3 and only Patrick Roy was the difference between a tie game and a steep Calgary lead. The Flames got to Roy in the second, scoring twice and heading to the final period up 2-0 on goals by Gilmour and Mullen. Montreal made it 2-1 midway through the third, but MacInnis made it 3-1. Claude Lemieux brought the Habs to within one with a goal at 19:33, but the Flames scored into the empty net and headed home with the series tied 2-2.

Game 5
May 23, 1989
Montreal 2 at **Calgary 3**

The Flames took control of the series with a commanding first period before a sold out house at the Saddledome, scoring just 28 seconds into the game (Otto) to get the game going and finishing the period with a 3-1 lead. Mike Keane scored for the

Habs in the second, but Mike Vernon's outstanding play in the final period made that 3-2 score hold up. As the teams headed back to Montreal for game six, Calgary was in a position to win the Stanley Cup.

Game 6
May 25, 1989
Calgary 4 at Montreal 2

There were a number of heroes on this night as the Flames won their first ever Stanley Cup and the Canadiens lost the Cup on home ice for their first time in their storied history. Colin Patterson scored the only goal of the first, but Claude Lemieux tied the game early in the second. Lanny McDonald broke the tie just three minutes later, realizing a dream by scoring in a Cup-clinching game. Doug Gilmour put the Flames up 3-1 midway through the third, and although Rick Green made the score 3-2 less than a minute later, the Flames hung on. Gilmour added his second goal of the period with an empty-net marker at 18:57, and the Calgary Flames won the Stanley Cup!

1989 CALGARY FLAMES PLAYOFF SCORING

#	Pos	Player	GP	G	A	P	Pim
2	D	Al MacInnis	22	7	24	31	46
7	F	Joe Mullen	21	16	8	24	4
39	F	Doug Gilmour	22	11	11	22	20
29	F	Joel Otto	22	6	13	19	46
12	F	Hakan Loob	22	8	9	17	4
25	F	Joe Nieuwendyk	22	10	4	14	10
11	F	Colin Patterson	22	3	10	13	24
10	F	Gary Roberts	22	5	7	12	57
55	D	Rob Ramage	20	1	11	12	26
14	F	Theo Fleury	22	5	6	11	24
34	D	Jamie Macoun	22	3	6	9	30
24	F	Jim Peplinski	20	1	6	7	75
27	F	Brian McLellan	21	3	2	5	19
22	F	Mark Hunter	10	2	2	4	23
9	F	Lanny McDonald	14	1	3	4	29
19	D	Tim Hunter	19	0	4	4	32
20	D	Gary Suter	5	0	3	3	10
6	D	Ric Nattress	19	0	3	3	20
5	D	Dana Murzyn	21	0	3	3	20
4	D	Brad McCrimmon	22	0	3	3	30
16	F	Sergei Priakin	1	0	0	0	0
23	D	Ken Sabourin	1	0	0	0	0
31	G	Rick Wamsley	1	0	0	0	0
17	F	Jiri Hrdina	4	0	0	0	0
30	G	Mike Vernon	22	0	0	0	14

Goalies

	GP	W-L	Mins	GA	SO	GAA
Mike Vernon	22	16-5	1,381	52	3	2.26
Rick Wamsley	1	0-1	20	2	0	6.00

Flames defenceman Al MacInnis receives the Conn Smythe Trophy as playoff MVP from NHL president John Ziegler.

Awards & Honours, Captains, Coaches & G.M's

ART ROSS TROPHY
Jarome Iginla, 2001-02

LESTER B. PEARSON AWARD
Jarome Iginla, 2001-02

"ROCKET" RICHARD TROPHY
Jarome Iginla, 2001-02
Jarome Iginla, 2003-04 (co-winner)

CONN SMYTHE TROPHY
Al MacInnis, 1988-89

CALDER TROPHY
Eric Vail, 1974-75 (Atlanta Flames)
Willi Plett, 1976-77
(Atlanta Flames)
Gary Suter, 1985-86
Joe Nieuwendyk, 1987-88
Sergei Makarov, 1989-90

BILL MASTERTON TROPHY
Lanny McDonald, 1982-83
Gary Roberts, 1995-96

LADY BYNG TROPHY
Bob MacMillan, 1978-79
(Atlanta Flames)
Joe Mullen, 1986-87
Joe Mullen, 1988-89

KING CLANCY AWARD
Lanny McDonald, 1987-88
Joe Nieuwendyk, 1994-95

CALGARY FLAMES
IN THE HOCKEY HALL OF FAME
(*year of induction in brackets following name*)
Glenn Hall (1975)
Goalie Consultant, 1988-2000

Bob Johnson (1992)
Head coach, 1982-1987

Guy Lapointe (1993)
Assistant coach & scout,
1990-1999

Lanny McDonald (1992)
Player, 1981-89; *Management*,
    1989-2000 & 2001-03

Joe Mullen (2000)
Player, 1985-1990

Grant Fuhr (2003)
Player, 1999-2000; *Goalie Consultant*,
    2000-2002

CALGARY FLAMES
RETIRED NUMBERS
9   Lanny McDonald

RALPH T. SCURFIELD HUMANITARIAN AWARD
annual award to the Flames player who "exemplifies the qualities of perseverance, determination, and leadership on the ice combined with dedication to community service"

1986-87	Lanny McDonald
1987-88	Jim Peplinski
1988-89	Lanny McDonald
1989-90	Tim Hunter
1990-91	Jamie Macoun
1991-92	Bob Johnson
1992-93	Joel Otto
1993-94	Al MacInnis
1994-95	not awarded
1995-96	Gary Roberts
1996-97	Mike Sullivan
1997-98	Ed Ward
1998-99	Ed Ward
1999-2000	Robyn Regehr
2000-01	Jarome Iginla
2001-02	Jarome Iginla
2002-03	Denis Gauthier
2003-04	Martin Gelinas

MOLSON CUP AWARDS

1980-81	Kent Nilsson
1981-82	Pat Riggin
1982-83	Lanny McDonald
1983-84	Rejean Lemelin
1984-85	Rejean Lemelin
1985-86	Hakan Loob
1986-87	Joe Mullen
1987-88	Hakan Loob
1988-89	Joe Mullen
1989-90	Joe Nieuwendyk
1990-91	Theo Fleury
1991-92	Mike Vernon
1992-93	Theo Fleury
1993-94	Joe Nieuwendyk
1994-95	Trevor Kidd
1995-96	Theo Fleury
1996-97	Trevor Kidd
1997-98	Theo Fleury
1998-99	Fred Brathwaite
1999-2000	Fred Brathwaite
2000-01	Jarome Iginla
2001-02	Jarome Iginla
2002-03	Jarome Iginla
2003-04	Jarome Iginla

CAPTAINS
Atlanta
Keith McCreary	1972-75
Pat Quinn	1975-77
Tom Lysiak	1977-79
Jean Pronovost	1979-80
Calgary
Brad Marsh	1980-81
Phil Russell	1981-83
Doug Risebrough	1983-87
Lanny McDonald	1983-89+
Jim Peplinski	1984-89+
Brad McCrimmon	1989-90
no captain	1990-91
Joe Nieuwendyk	1991-95
Theo Fleury	1995-97
Todd Simpson	1997-99
Steve Smith	1999-2000
Dave Lowry	2000-02+
Bob Boughner	2000-03+
Craig Conroy	2002-2003
Jarome Iginla	2003-present
+co-captains	

CALGARY FLAMES ALL-STAR TEAM SELECTIONS
Lanny McDonald,
1982-83, right wing, 2nd team
Al MacInnis,
1986-87, defence, 2nd team
Brad McCrimmon,
1987-88, defence, 2nd team
Gary Suter,
1987-88, defence, 2nd team
Hakan Loob,
1987-88, right wing, 1st team
Mike Vernon,
1988-89, goal, 2nd team
Al MacInnis,
1988-89, defence, 2nd team
Joe Mullen,
1988-89, right wing, 1st team
Al MacInnis,
1989-90, defence, 1st team
Al MacInnis,
1990-91, defence, 1st team
Al MacInnis,
1993-94, defence, 2nd team
Theo Fleury,
1994-95, right wing, 2nd team
Jarome Iginla,
2001-02, right wing, 1st team

GENERAL MANAGERS
Cliff Fletcher
1972-1991

Doug Risebrough
May 16, 1991-November 3, 1995

Al Coates
November 3, 1995-April 11, 2000

Craig Button
June 6, 2000-April 11, 2003

Darryl Sutter
April 11, 2003-present

COACHES' RECORDS

YEAR	COACH	REGULAR SEASON				PLAYOFFS		
		GP	W	L	T	W	L	PO
1972-73	Bernie Geoffrion	78	25	38	15		DNQ	
1973-74	Bernie Geoffrion	78	30	34	14	0	4	0-1
1974-75	Bernie Geoffrion	52	22	20	10	—	—	—
	Fred Creighton	28	12	11	5		DNQ	
1975-76	Fred Creighton	80	35	33	12	0	2	0-1
1976-77	Fred Creighton	80	34	34	12	1	2	0-1
1977-78	Fred Creighton	80	34	27	19	0	2	0-1
1978-79	Fred Creighton	80	41	31	8	0	2	0-1
1979-80	Al MacNeil	80	35	32	13	1	3	0-1
1980-81	Al MacNeil	80	39	27	14	9	7	2-1
1981-82	Al MacNeil	80	29	34	17	0	3	0-1
1982-83	Bob Johnson	80	32	34	14	4	5	1-1
1983-84	Bob Johnson	80	34	32	14	6	5	1-1
1984-85	Bob Johnson	80	41	27	12	1	3	0-1
1985-86	Bob Johnson	80	40	31	9	12	10	3-1
1986-87	Bob Johnson	80	46	31	3	2	4	0-1
1987-88	Terry Crisp	80	48	23	9	4	5	1-1
1988-89	Terry Crisp	80	54	17	9	16	6	4-0
1989-90	Terry Crisp	80	42	23	15	2	4	0-1
1990-91	Doug Risebrough	80	46	26	8	3	4	0-1
1991-92	Doug Risebrough	64	25	30	9	—	—	—
	Guy Charron	16	6	7	3		DNQ	
1992-93	Dave King	84	43	30	11	2	4	0-1
1993-94	Dave King	84	42	29	13	3	4	0-1
1994-95	Dave King	48	24	17	7	3	4	0-1
1995-96	Pierre Page	82	34	37	11	0	4	0-1
1996-97	Pierre Page	82	32	41	9		DNQ	
1997-98	Brian Sutter	82	26	41	15		DNQ	
1998-99	Brian Sutter	82	30	40	12		DNQ	
1999-2000	Brian Sutter	82	31	36	10(5)		DNQ	
2000-01	Don Hay	68	23	28	13(4)	—	—	—
	Greg Gilbert	14	4	8	2(0)		DNQ	
2001-02	Greg Gilbert	82	32	35	12(3)		DNQ	
2002-03	Greg Gilbert	25	6	13	3(3)	—	—	—
	Al MacNeil	11	4	5	2(0)	—	—	—
	Darryl Sutter	46	19	18	8(1)		DNQ	
2003-04	Darryl Sutter	82	42	30	7(3)	15	11	3-4